Breakthrough Prayer

Steven Anderson

New Wine Press

New Wine Press
PO Box 17
Chichester
England PO20 6YB

Unless otherwise stated, Scripture quotations are from the New
International Version of the Bible, © 1978 New York International Bible
Society. Published by Hodder & Stoughton.

ISBN: 1-903725-23-2

Typeset by CRB Associates, Reepham, Norfolk.
Printed in England by Clays Ltd, St Ives plc.

Contents

Introduction

Prayer is a most amazing privilege and a most powerful weapon. Yet because of this, it can be an incredible struggle.

Over the years the Lord has increasingly impressed upon me the importance of developing a life of prayer. In more recent times he has called my wife, Helen, and me to lead a prayer ministry in our city, and to call the Church to 'invest in prayer'.

There are different types of prayer – for example, devotional, meditation, intercession, and it is important to recognise the type of prayer in which we are seeking to engage. In much prayer we are looking for God's response – but it does not always appear to come. When we engage in conversation with someone we expect them to reply, and if they don't we tend to be put off talking to them. Prayer is conversation with God; it is a two-way communication. Yet most of us have felt that we have often done most of the talking. Now part of the problem – a big part – may be our inability to listen well. My daughters sometimes speak to me telling me all sorts of things. The conversation seems to be going well until they ask a question and fail to get a meaningful answer. At this point they discern that I have not been giving them my full attention. Likewise we may be talking to God but not really expecting any answer or giving much attention to what he might be saying.

However, it is hard to keep up a one-sided conversation, and if we are honest our prayers can seem that way much of the time. Yet God longs to respond to us, and is responding more often than we think. Two great needs that we have are, first of all to learn to listen to God, and second to persevere in prayer when there does not seem to be any immediate response. A clear lesson from Scripture and history is this – perseverance pays. We see this in the ministry of Elijah when he sends his servant seven times to go and look for the sign of the coming rain (1 Kings 18:43, 44). Naaman likewise had to dip seven times in the river in order to be cleansed of his leprosy (2 Kings 5). Abraham had to wait until his old age to see the child of promise come from Sarah's womb, and David had to wait fourteen years from Samuel's anointing and prophecy concerning him before becoming king. Many of the stories we hear of great breakthrough in the world today have been preceded by years, even decades, of faithful, persevering prayer.

In this book we want to think mostly about intercessory prayer which, simply put, is asking God to act on behalf of others, and to pray for his purposes to be worked out on earth as in heaven. For much more detailed definitions of intercessory prayer I would recommend *Intercessory Prayer* by Dutch Sheets.

Forms of intercessory prayer

In my prayer journey I have found the following three categories of intercessory prayer to be helpful. There are several other categories that could be used, but these three help differentiate them in a way that is useful for our study.

1. Apostolic intercession
By this I mean praying the prayers that the apostles prayed in the New Testament, for example Paul's prayers for the church at Ephesus found in Ephesians 1:17–19 and 3:16–19. These, and indeed other biblical prayers, are most useful and necessary for us to keep praying. We can be confident that God

agrees with these prayers, and the apostolic prayers highlight the key needs for the Church in all ages. I have made this type of praying a regular and continual practice in my life and in corporate prayer meetings.

2. Prophetic intercession
I use this term for prayer where the Holy Spirit prompts us through visions, dreams, prophecies and so forth, to pray and ask for something to be accomplished that is on God's heart for the present time. For example, in one prayer meeting a friend of ours saw in a vision an orphanage run by Catholic nuns which she perceived was in Rwanda. We were, she believed, to pray for their protection. Not knowing anything more, and with this not being in our minds previously to her seeing this vision, we believed this was a prophetic prompt of the Holy Spirit and prayed accordingly. A few days later I saw on the BBC news the story of a Rwandan orphanage run by Catholic sisters where armed guerrillas had arrived, but left again without harming anyone.

In the apostolic prayers we ask for *'the Spirit of wisdom and revelation'* (Ephesians 1:17) and should therefore surely expect God to give that to us.

3. Persevering intercession
By this term I mean praying for other people, situations, churches, our town, city or nation, where there has been no direct revelation from the Spirit, but where we are praying in accordance with the general will and purposes of God to save, heal and set people free. The apostolic prayers require perseverance, but they are clearly for the continual growth and building up of the Church. Prophetic prayers may also require some perseverance at times, but there is a sense that God has told us to pray this and he will respond. The prayers we are now referring to may require much perseverance, even for many years, such as praying for the salvation of a family member or praying for revival in our locality.

This book is divided into three sections. In the first I shall relate something of our story along with principles that the

Lord has taught us. In the second section the focus will be on overcoming the obstacles to persevering in prayer, looking at three passages of Scripture where a parent came to Jesus desperately concerned for a son or daughter. In his teaching Jesus clearly encouraged persevering prayer (see Luke 11:5–13; 18:1–7). In the final section I shall present the case for prioritising prayer in our lives and in our churches, with chapters containing some thoughts on having dynamic prayer meetings and the need to get prayer out of the Church.

God desires to see his children breaking through in prayer. If we learn what he is teaching us through the Word and put this into practice, and if we give prayer a true place of priority in our lives and in our churches then we will see remarkable breakthroughs.

SECTION 1

God's Call

Chapter 1

Bridges and Canopies of Prayer

The adventure begins

In 1987 I was inducted as the Pastor of a small Baptist church on a very large housing estate on the south side of Glasgow. Helen and I had both sensed that the Lord had guided us quite clearly to go there, and the task was to equip the believers and lead the church forward in reaching out to the local community. It did not take long for me to realise that the task was beyond my ability, and that I desperately needed God's help.

I became increasingly aware of the need to develop my own prayer life, especially learning how to listen to the Father, and found that I began having dreams that were very different from my usual dreams, and were often very vivid. I suspect that God will communicate with us in whatever way he wants, and that my active lifestyle meant that when I slept was probably the only time I was still enough. Sometimes the meaning of the dreams was reasonably clear, relating to a current ministry situation, and at other times the meaning was more obscure, drawing me to spend more time seeking the Lord for the interpretation and application of the dream.

In 1990 a group of us from the church attended a conference where we heard Mike Bickle from Kansas City speak on intercessory prayer. I had not heard of Bickle before this but was struck both by his obvious passion and the content of his teaching. Our response as a church was to begin two prayer meetings – Monday and Saturday evenings – and take up the call to cry out for an outpouring of the Holy Spirit on our area. Though there was often only a small group of around six to twelve of us, these became very special times where we often sensed the Spirit of God moving powerfully and wonderfully among us. Indeed this sense of his immediate presence and anointing sustained us as a small group in the face of many other discouraging factors.

After some time we did drop the Saturday meeting and moved the Monday night one into the church building. Here we found the Holy Spirit led us on quite an adventure of prayer. I have been in many places where there has been a strong moving of the Spirit, yet rarely experienced anything like that little group experienced some Monday evenings on a Glasgow housing estate. The Lord led us into more intimate worship, caused us to be still at times to listen to him, and led us to pray for situations for which we would never have thought to pray. One example was to pray for Albania. Helen had received a call from the Lord one morning – while in the shower – to pray for Albania. Geography not being her strong point she had no idea where this country was located, nor did she know anything about it. As we began to pray for this little nation a great anointing would fall upon the intercessors. Soon Albania became familiar as the troubles from this land began to appear on our television screens, and we realised why God had led us to pray for that nation. A group from the church went first to Italy to the refugee camps, then the next year into Albania where they linked up with a wonderful church there.

The Lord is looking for people who will listen to him and obey the prompting of his Spirit, to pray what he tells them to, and to follow those prayers with any appropriate action. We do not need to be a big church, or have a strong dynamic prayer ministry, but just two or three obedient believers, open to the Holy Spirit's leading, can pray in powerful and life-changing ways.

Around this time I began to get involved in citywide prayer meetings, and found the Lord gradually lifting my eyes to see a whole city and not just 'our corner of the vineyard'. God was leading us on an adventure of prayer and would call us to step out in ways we would not have foreseen.

Dream of a city clothed in light

A key in the forming of this vision in my life was the dreams. One night I dreamt that I was standing on a high piece of ground looking over to a city that was clothed in the most brilliant light. As I looked more closely though, I could see that all the houses had their doors closed and shutters down over the outside of the windows so that none of the light was entering the homes. I had the sense that all that was needed was for someone to go over and lift the shutters, and this wonderful light would flood each house. Then I saw that between the city and me was a deep gorge that I could not get across.

As I sought the Lord concerning this matter I sensed him say that the only way across this gorge was to build a bridge of prayer. I believe that if we build these 'bridges of prayer' then through the intercessory work the blinding influences of Satan will be lifted off the people and the work of the harvest will become so much easier and more fruitful.

There appears to be a tension at times between those who emphasise the need to pray for revival and those who say we need to get out there and make Jesus known. I do not think there needs to be any tension over this as we desperately need both, but I think it is vital that we prepare the way for the work of evangelism with a significant level of prayer.

The call to prayer was becoming well imprinted in my spirit.

Called to be a 'bridgehead'

On another occasion while I was praying alone in the church building I sensed the voice of God speak quite clearly into my inner being and say, 'you are to be a bridgehead'. I was not sure exactly what the term meant, but guessed that if I were to build a bridge of prayer then a 'bridgehead' would be of significance. My dictionary defines 'bridgehead' as a 'post held on far side of river giving one access to enemy's position'. I did not sense the Lord say I was to build or form a bridgehead, but that I was to be a bridgehead.

Some years afterwards, with the release of the *Transformations* videos, I heard George Otis Jr speak of beachheads – key points of ground in enemy territory that establish a position through which your army can invade the land. Beachheads and bridgeheads are very similar in their purpose and function.

The meaning of this in my life would become clearer as God moved me from the pastoral ministry to lead a citywide prayer ministry.

Vision for the Canopy

In October 1998 I took some sabbatical time out to seek the Lord and wait on him for any instructions or words for the church. This was a refreshing time with the opportunity to speak and minister in several other churches. It was also good to have days doing nothing other than seek God in prayer. I expected that he might give me some new word of direction for the church but nothing came. I felt a bit disappointed, even rather miffed, but God was leading me in a new direction altogether, one that my dull mind had not yet grasped.

At the very end of those two months I had a vision. It was nothing too dramatic, and was over in seconds. I was not even praying at the time but was waiting to collect one of my daughters. In the vision I 'saw' a very muddy field with people trying to walk through it but they would slip and fall back. Some people put in planks of wood, which helped a little, but soon they became covered in mud and very slippery. That was it. Then I sensed the Holy Spirit drop a question into my thoughts – 'What is the problem here?' My immediate response was that the mud was the problem. He gently corrected me as I sensed him suggest it was the rain that makes the mud that was the real problem. My mind seemed to be opened up and I realised that what was needed was a canopy to cover the field.

I believed this vision had been a picture of the harvest field, with new believers struggling to move forward in the Christian walk, and often slipping back. The planks of wood represented the many good initiatives that can help young disciples to grow, but even these began to lose their effectiveness. The need was to provide a shelter from what the evil one sends, and that shelter needed to be a canopy of prayer.

The following year we launched just such a Prayer Canopy for our city with churches of many different denominations taking one day a month to pray a covering over the city. I believe the full impact and importance of this canopy is still to come in the days when we will see a greater harvest for the Kingdom of God. We need to raise up the cry of intercessory prayer that will usher in a Holy Spirit awakening to our land, but we need to remember to keep up a continual watch and covering of prayer that the harvest will be maintained and not quickly spoiled or lost. The danger is that we would in such a time become so busy with the works of evangelism and discipling that we let slip our vigilance in prayer. Once that guard is down the enemy will not be slow to come to wreak havoc with the tender shoots.

Start of Prayer for the City in Glasgow

Having launched the Prayer Canopy the Lord soon launched Helen and me out into the prayer ministry on a full-time basis. It had become increasingly obvious to all around us that this was the way God was leading us, yet he still had to push me out of the door of pastoral ministry by making things increasingly difficult. My biggest surprise was that nobody else seemed surprised at the change of direction.

At the end of 1999 we moved ahead with Prayer for the City in Glasgow, bringing together the existing Canopy of Prayer and leaders' prayer meetings, and setting up a Prayer Wall[1] and other initiatives with the aim of seeing continual prayer sustained for our city.

One key passage of Scripture in forming the vision of this ministry was **Isaiah 62**. The opening verse speaks of the Lord's passion for his people. I believe this to be the Lord Jesus' cry for the Church in this day – *that our righteousness will shine out, and salvation will go forth from us like a blazing torch*. This is the Lord's heart cry and must become ours too. In order for that to truly happen something needs to happen to us:

A new name (Isaiah 2b–5)

The Lord says he will call us by a new name – his mouth will bestow or place this name upon us. A name in Scripture is indicative of character. God is giving to us a new character, that of his Son. It is not something we work up, earn or deserve. This is a work of grace, of divine favour. In these days God is bestowing this to his Church. He is highlighting the revelation of the scriptural truth of who we are in Christ, and of his delight in us. It is only in the understanding of this that we will have the confidence and the strength to fulfil his wonderful purposes for us in these times. As we come into the greater understanding of the revelation of his love for us, and the knowledge that he actually delights in us as a bridegroom delights in his bride, so we are freed from our striving, and instead desire to spend more time in his presence. It is as we spend time beholding him that he changes us into the likeness of Christ (2 Corinthians 3:18). I will expand this theme in chapter 3.

The truth is that God looks at you as his child through the blood of Christ. He delights in you, not because of your maturity or works of service, but because of the fact that you are his son or daughter. Normally parents will love and adore their newborn baby. The baby cannot serve the parents, and is not in any way mature. In fact this child will cause their parents considerable work, disturbed sleep, and much inconvenience. Yet it is all worth it for the joy that the baby brings to their lives. Now they will want the child to grow, mature and live a useful life. So our Heavenly Father wants us to grow and mature, and he does want us to serve him and bear fruit, but his love for us does not depend on our success at these things.

I believe we do not live in the freedom that Christ made available for us until we grasp this revelation of his delighting in us. Realising his delight will draw us into increased worship and prayer, not out of any sense of guilt if we do not spend time in these pursuits, but out of a growing desire to be with the Lover of our souls.

Isaiah 62:4 speaks of the name change – no longer *'Deserted'* and *'Desolate'*, but *'Hephzibah'* meaning his delight is in her, and *'Beulah'* meaning married. Our lives may have felt deserted at times when it seemed God was not very close to us. Some of our churches have literally been deserted and desolate with buildings closing down. God desires to change things – to bring us into an intimate relationship with Jesus, to know him as our bridegroom. When the Church comes more fully into this knowledge we will glow like newly wed brides who know the delight of their husbands. This glow will attract people to us. No longer will the Church be deserted or desolate, but instead our *'sheep will increase by thousands, by tens of thousands in our fields'* (Psalm 144:13). When our lives, and our lives together as the Church, display this new name, this new character, the world will see the true grace and love of the Lord, which is what so many search for in all the wrong places.

So as we enter more deeply into a marriage with Jesus Christ we will see God rejoicing over us. It is such an amazing thought that Almighty God rejoices over you and me. Zephaniah 3:17 describes this beautifully:

> *'The LORD your God is with you,*
> *he is mighty to save.*
> *He will take great delight in you,*
> *he will quiet you with his love,*
> *he will rejoice over you with singing.'*

A new level of prayer (Isaiah 62:6–7)

The reason for the ministry of Prayer for the City, and the reason for this book, is that we do not believe this is a day for ordinary prayer, but for extraordinary prayer. God is calling for a new level of prayer from his people. We see this all over the world today.

In order to be able to step up to this new level, both in the quantity of our prayers, and the quality of our prayers, we need to know the delight of the Lord. We need to experience what he promised for his house of prayer in Isaiah 56:7, namely that he would give us joy in prayer. It is the intimacy, the knowledge of his delight in us, the learning to delight in him, and express that delight back to him, that will release us into this joy. In turn the joy will sustain us in prayer, and even propel us on to new levels. Prayer can be hard work at times, and there is a danger that we can feel that prayer can be a drudge rather than a delight.

The Lord says in these verses that he has posted watchman on the walls. These watchmen are to continue in prayer night and day, giving neither themselves, nor the Lord, any rest until he fulfils his promise.

(a) Positioned by the Lord

It is not our idea to be watchmen. It is God's initiative and his calling to us. If we just decided this ourselves we would fail to reach the level of intercessory prayer that is required. However, God is calling many people in the Church to a new level of prayer in these days. This is in preparation for a coming move of the Spirit of God that will sweep multitudes into the Kingdom. The position of a watchman on the wall is not only about calling out in prayer, but about watching and listening. We need to look and see what the Lord is doing, and what the enemy is up to, and also listen and hear what the Spirit is saying. For this task we need an observant spirit to be developed in us, the sort of awareness that caused Moses to observe that a bush was on fire (not uncommon in the desert) yet did not burn up. Proverbs 8:34 describes this observant one who listens to the Lord, *'watching daily at my doors, waiting at my doorway.'* Having seen and heard, the watchman will cry out for God to fulfil what he has revealed, giving due warning of what the enemy is seeking to do and praying protection on the Church and the harvest.

(b) Day and night prayer

This concept is being developed quite literally in many places today through the formation of prayer walls (usually 7×24 one-hour slots) and other initiatives. The example of the Moravians and their famous prayer tower at Herrnhut has been an inspiration to many of us. This relatively small group of believers living on the estate of Count Zinzendorf manned this prayer tower continuously for over 100 years, and also sent missionaries to some of the most difficult places on the earth, several of them laying down their lives for the gospel.[2]

While we must not get hung up in a legalistic manner about having 24-hour prayer going on every day, the general concept of this scripture is important for us to see revival and transformation come to our towns, cities and nations.

Why is day and night prayer important?
1.   God calls for it (Isaiah 62:6–7; Luke 18:7–8; Leviticus 6:12–13).
2.   It is the pattern of heaven (Revelation 4:8).
3.   The harvest requires it – praying it in and continually covering it (1 Thessalonians 5:17; Ephesians 6:18; Colossians 4:2–3).
4.   Our enemy never rests (1 Peter 5:8; Revelation 12:10).

I believe the Lord would have us 'take back the night'. So often we associate the natural darkness of the night with the spiritually dark activities of sin. The night appears to be the time for much satanic activity, immorality, drunkenness and so on. The truth is God created the day and the night, and God often acts at night in significant ways. The Scriptures give many incidences of God acting, delivering and speaking to people at night.[3] We read of Joshua going up against the five kings of the Amorites who had attacked Gibeon. Joshua 10:9 says, *'After an all-night march from Gilgal, Joshua took them by surprise.'* This led to a great victory for the army of Israel. We can similarly take the enemy by surprise and win great victories when we give ourselves to new levels of extraordinary prayer.

A new day of victory (Isaiah 62:8–9)

The result of increased prayer will be this new day of victory over the enemy. The Israelites went through times where they were oppressed by enemies and raided by them, losing the harvest for which they had worked hard. They would then cry out to the Lord who would respond in mercy by raising up a deliverer. We read of one such time in Judges 6–8 where the Midianites and other peoples raided Israel, and the Lord raised up Gideon to bring about a miraculous deliverance for his people.

Too often the Church has seemed oppressed rather than walking in the liberty of Christ. Too often the enemy has ravaged the little harvest that we have reaped. It is only through a significant increase of prayer that we will see the new day of victory come, a day in which the Church will walk in freedom and the power of the Holy Spirit. It is only when we get the prayer cover in place that we will reap and keep the wonderful harvest that God intends for us.

New doors for the good news (Isaiah 62:10)

With the new name upon the Church, the *'delighted in'* people of God crying out to him day and night, and the enemy being defeated and held at bay by the sheer volume of intercession, new doors will open wide for the good news to go forth. This is our goal – to make Jesus known in all the earth. Though spending time in God's Presence is worthwhile in itself, we do not pray just for the sake of praying, but for the sake of fulfilling the commission he has given to us. While we do need to get things in order – it is vital to have the love relationship with God as a primary focus of our lives – but out of this relationship his love will flow in us. Such love will inevitably cause us to reach out to the lost and needy around us.

Prayer will remove the blinding influences of the evil one and break down the ungodly mindsets that set themselves up against the knowledge of God. Yet we still have a responsibility to go through the doors and clear the obstacles out of the way. Sadly many of the obstacles to people coming to Christ have been put there by the Church – by disunity and schism, by holding on to outdated and unbiblical practices, and by the lack of Christ-likeness in our lives. We must remove these 'stones' and raise up the banner of Christ. As we develop citywide unity, encourage forgiving attitudes in the Body of Christ, and grow in our knowledge of his love we will remove some obstacles. We also need to find new expressions for being Church so that we can raise the banner in ways and in places where people can see it. (We will come to this in the next chapter.)

Another word of Isaiah helps sum up the message of this chapter:

> *'This is what the Lord says:*
> *"In the time of my favour I will answer you,*
>   *and in the day of salvation I will help you;*
> *I will keep you and will make you*
>   *to be a covenant for the people,*
> *to restore the land*
>   *and to reassign its desolate inheritances,*
> *to say to the captives, 'Come out,'*
>   *and to those in darkness, 'Be free!'''* '   (Isaiah 49:8–9a)

The time of God's favour is upon us, but how can he answer us if we do not ask of him? We must not let his favour drift by us, but call on him, and ask with great boldness and determination, so that we will receive his answers and his help. Then we will set the captives free and change our land in his name.

Notes

1. Many cities and areas of the country have set up Prayer Walls. These initiatives usually involve people signing up to pray for the same hour every week, connecting by telephone with 'the watchmen' on either side of their time slot.
2. See *The Lost Art of Intercession*, Jim Goll (Destiny Image, 1997).
3. See for example Genesis 26:24; 32:22ff.; Exodus 12; 14:21; Judges 6:25; 1 Samuel 3; Psalm 16:7; 42:8; Luke 6:12; Acts 16:9; 16:25; 18:9.

Chapter 2

The Four 'R's and Four Aims

I woke in the middle of one night with the clear impression of a voice saying to me, 'Isaiah 58:12.' That was all, just the Scripture reference. I knew the chapter fairly well as we had prayed through it and sought to act on it in our church on a few occasions. I was not sure exactly what verse 12 said but eagerly looked it up.

> *'Your people will rebuild the ancient ruins*
> *and will raise up the age-old foundations;*
> *You will be called Repairer of Broken Walls,*
> *Restorer of Streets with Dwellings.'*

This verse contains four key action terms – **rebuild**, **raise up**, **repair**, and **restore**. This was what needed to be done in Jerusalem and what needs to be done in our cities too. The concepts of this verse could be applied in various ways. In our city of Glasgow there is a need to rebuild the ancient ruins of the Christian heritage that came to our area, first through Celtic missionaries. They brought the gospel along with an emphasis on prayer cells, the prophetic gifts, the miraculous works of God, and recognition of spiritual warfare. We need to rebuild the Church that knows the voice of the Lord and how to move in the power of the Holy Spirit.

Our city was founded on a wonderful prayer:

'O Lord, let Glasgow flourish
By the preaching of Thy Word
And the praising of Thy Name.'

This is our age-old foundation, one that we are seeking to raise up once again. Long ago the civil authorities of our city cut this motto to 'Let Glasgow flourish'. The city will only truly flourish through prayer, the preaching of the good news of Jesus Christ, and the praising of his glorious name.

The broken walls of the Church need to be repaired – the walls of prayer, the walls of defence that kept the enemy out. We are seeking to do this with continual prayer cover over the city. Likewise there needs to be a restoration of streets with dwellings, that is the provision of homes where people can be sheltered, nurtured and build relationships. It is the Church that provides such a home and therefore the Church needs to be restored in all the fullness of the ministry and gifts that Christ gave to her.

City transformation

Not long after launching out in Prayer for the City we came across the video called *Transformations* produced by the Sentinel Group. This was a huge encouragement and inspiration, proving to be a powerful tool in explaining our vision for the transformation of our city. We had some strange battles showing this video in churches where video players or television sets would suddenly stop working when they had worked fine beforehand. Once I had to sit with my hand on the video player and keep praying over it until the tape had been shown! Drawing on this and other resources, we began to formulate and express our aims.

The key focus of our prayers is for the transformation of our city through:

1. the renewal of the Church
2. a spiritual awakening in the city leading to many conversions

3.   major godly changes in our society, e.g. reduction in crime, freedom from addictions, breakdown of sectarianism, and other changes that our city needs in order to become a godlier place.

We believe that Jesus' ministry was about transforming lives, freeing people from the power of sin, the oppression of demonic forces and the crippling effect of sickness, and bringing them into a new life of fullness. One great example of this in Luke's Gospel is in chapter 13:10–13 where we find Jesus setting free and healing a poor crippled woman. A spirit had crippled the woman for eighteen years. Many in our towns and cities are similarly oppressed by the powers of darkness, and crippled by the wounds inflicted on their lives through abuse, divorce, loss and much more. Like this woman they can be set free from their infirmity by the authoritative word of Jesus, and healed by the touching of his hands. They too can be transformed so that they 'straighten up and praise God'.

We believe that this can happen not only for certain individuals but also for whole communities.

What then are the means by which this wonderful transformation will come? God will work as he chooses and may work quite differently in one situation than he does in another. It is troubling that so many seem to run after the latest formula for Church growth and success, instead of seeking God and hearing from him, while gleaning principles that will help from those who have travelled a similar road. There appears from *Transformations* and other accounts to be a couple of key principles that are most important. We have adopted these (1 and 2 below) along with two other key aims for the ministry in our city.

The aims of Prayer for the City

1. To facilitate persevering, united, envisioned leadership in our city

In 1996 some church leaders on the south side of Glasgow

began to meet to pray together and pray for each other. This small group from a variety of churches soon developed a strong bond in prayer. We knew that we could easily stay a small group with a deepening relationship, but that God's will for us was to open up and bring others to join us. The group has grown over the years, signing a covenant of our commitment to the Lord, to his purpose for the city, and to one another. We have an annual retreat where we worship and seek the Lord together, and at this time relationships deepen all the more.

It is important that such a group does not meet just because it seems a nice idea, nor should we see unity in itself as our goal. The three adjectives below all need to be included in a true description of the type of church leadership we must see developed in the city.

Persevering

When I was at college training for the pastoral ministry I got the impression that most ministers would go to a church they felt called to, spend a few years there (about 3–5 years if it was a small church, maybe 7–8 years if it was a bigger church), then move on to the next place in God's call. Among the advantages of moving about were that you were less likely to grow stale, you gained wider experience, and you could use the same set of sermons in the next place! There were costs too, especially to children having to move town and school. In recent times I see a trend where ministers are staying longer in their churches and showing a commitment to their community. This is a most welcome trend. Provided those involved can remain fresh, longer term ministries bring greater stability, an increased ability to build the local church, and the opportunity to build the city Church with strong relationships among the leaders of congregations. I believe such perseverance has two other key advantages. First I think that often ministers have moved on when things were tough not knowing that a real breakthrough may have just been around the corner. Breakthroughs often come after the hardest and most testing times. Second our commitment to persevere in our church and area speaks powerfully to the forces of the enemy in our locality. The evil one and his demons can work to keep a ministry at bay for a time, and will seek to wear you out, discourage you and get you out their territory, but our statement and act of perseverance will conquer the plans of the enemy.[1]

As we have built up a praying relationship among church leaders in Glasgow it has been a great strength that a core number are those with long-term ministry commitments in our city.

United

It is vital that we are persevering together in our area with the aim of building the Kingdom of God. We need unity among leaders and in our churches. Most people recognise this as God's will – it is where 'he commands his blessing', and it is the answer to Jesus' prayer of John 17. The value of a united Church is fairly clear – shared resources, the way we look to those outside the Church, power of agreement in prayer and so on. It is not that anyone really says unity is a bad thing, but there are a couple of cautions that are raised.

One is concerned with where we draw the boundary lines of unity. Some churches are happy to participate in interfaith events with Muslims, Hindus and other major religions. Most within the evangelical wing of the Church would not go to that length, but see that as a serious compromise. On the other hand there are those who will not participate in anything with those who do not hold the same doctrine as them in almost every matter. A standard middle ground has been that we need to agree on the essentials, such as the person of Christ, his death and resurrection and so forth, while we can amicably hold different views on secondary issues such as the mode of baptism or means of church government. Of course some may disagree as to what is essential and what is secondary.

Unity has also been established at times on agreement of style, that is we meet and pray with those with whom we feel comfortable. I believe we can move forward in unity with those who love the Lord as their personal Saviour, acknowledging him as the unique Son of God, acknowledge the authority of the Scriptures, and have a desire to pray together for the Kingdom of God to come in their community. Francis Frangipane, a well-known author and speaker on city reaching strategies, speaks of 'that living, united, praying church in the city. The Lord's house will consist of evangelicals and Pentecostals, traditional churches and charismatics; it will be free of racial and class prejudices. They will simply be Christians who know Jesus as Lord, believe the truth of the Scriptures and are committed to one another as brethren. Although they will continue to maintain their national affiliations, they will be uniquely anointed to bring healing to their cities.' [2]

Rather than fearing those who do not hold to the exact same doctrine as ourselves, we need to be open to humbly relate and pray together that God might lead us on in his will and purpose.

The second cautionary note is the concern that unity in any way implies uniformity. It most certainly does not. In fact God has so created our world that it is full of beauty caused by the different shapes, textures and colours that we see all around us. I believe he has created his Church in the same way – full of variety.

In the family there is to be the family likeness (hopefully a Christ-likeness), but also great diversity. This is the wonder of his grace. This is the way the body works, with all the different parts doing their work in submission to the head. Otherwise we might look very dull. We need to see a variety of expressions of the gifts that God bestows upon his Church, and we need a variety of types or styles of church in our city. One size does not fit all.

Envisioned

We may persevere and we may have a lovely sense of unity among us, but without a vision from the Lord we will never reach our community. It is quite possible to start well but stop well short. This can happen in a town or city where the church leaders come together in unity with every intention of praying and working together for the godly transformation of their area, but without realising it they get stuck at the unity stage. That is, they begin to enjoy the unity and become content with that, or they have mistakenly made unity their goal, or they are afraid to move forward in case they jeopardise the unity they have worked so hard to achieve.

We must not stop short. We must be leaders who are hearing from the Lord and getting hold of his vision for our community. Most leaders have a visionary side to their make up. They will hopefully have a vision for their own local fellowship, but often have little vision for their town or city, or fear sharing it in case they are seen as presumptuous. We can sit back waiting on someone else to take the initiative. It is essential that we recognise leaders among leaders, those with an apostolic function to bring ministries together and thrust them forward, and bring a message and anointing for breakthrough in our land.

Leaders' groupings also tend to be comprised predominantly of those with a pastoral or teaching ministry. I greatly value these ministries, but feel there has been an imbalance in the Church for centuries. We need the apostolic, prophetic and evangelistic ministries to come forth in our cities and nations. In groups that are principally pastors/teachers we desperately need to make room for the prophetic voice, and the stirring of the evangelist. Christ gave a five-fold ministry gifting to the Church (Ephesians 4:11–12) and we need the balance of all these ministries functioning together. Only then will we come forth as the mature Body of Christ that can truly bring transformation to our communities.

I believe that it is important for gatherings of church leaders to maintain a sharpness and width at the same time. This is not an easy thing to do. Some gatherings could be sharp and focused, yet remain fairly exclusive, with the unspoken signal of 'you have to pray like us to fit in here'. Other groups could be very welcoming, embracing people from all manner of church style. These groups can fall into the danger of never really doing anything because they are afraid to offend anyone. They have looked for the lowest common denominator and do not mention anything beyond it. I have been in meetings of church leaders where the suggestion of praying together clearly caused embarrassment!

I believe we can, and must, find the grace to have leaders' gatherings that are sharp and focused, making headway in enacting the vision God gives, but at the same time display a humble attitude that embraces those who think and speak a little different but still love the Lord and seek his Kingdom.

2. To encourage sustained, united, fervent prayer

We used the title 'Prayer for the City' in order to emphasise the priority of prayer that we believe is necessary in fulfilling our commission. We do believe that we need to do much more than pray as we reach out to the people of our city. However, prayer is vital in preparing the way for and sustaining other ministry. Francis Frangipane says, 'Corporate, heartfelt, citywide prayer for our communities and our nation is the most essential dynamic for seeing our society turned and our cities redeemed.'[3]

We aim therefore to encourage the Church to pray, and to pray in the above ways. We could add a number of other adjectives to our list – humble, repentant, believing, bold, Spirit-inspired and so on. These are all good and necessary but here we want to emphasise these three.

Sustained

If we are to see our city transformed in any significant way then it won't just happen overnight. It will require sustained battling prayer. It can be easy to pray for a short time. It can be most encouraging to bring a need before the Lord and see his answer soon follow. To pray for a changed community is not so easy. To turn a small rowing boat around only requires a few feet of water, but to turn an ocean going liner may require miles. Turning the direction of a city requires a long-term commitment. There will be many trials and tests, and times when we feel that God is not listening, far less answering. The key at such times is to be honest about how we feel – David did this regularly in the Psalms – and then to press on all the more. As we set ourselves to take ground from the enemy he will come against us even quite fiercely at times. The key for us is to keep on steadfastly stating our commitment to pray for transformation.

Our intention is to seek to provide encouragement and strength to the praying people of our city, that we might hold up each other's arms before the throne of grace.

United

I have covered much on this point in (1) above, but would emphasise the tremendous power and value of praying in agreement. In Matthew 18:19 Jesus says, *'Again, I tell you that if two of you on earth agree about anything you ask for, it will be done for you by my Father in heaven.'* And the principle of this power of agreement is brought out in Leviticus 26:8, *'Five of you will chase a hundred, and a hundred of you will chase ten thousand.'* The normal laws of multiplication would mean that a hundred (20×5) should chase twenty times the hundred, that is two thousand, but instead will chase ten thousand (100×100). The influence of two praying together will not be the sum of the two (individuals or churches), but a far greater amount.

Fervent

While perseverance is vital to prayer, and unity gives much added strength, it is important that we are also fervent in prayer. My dictionary defines 'fervent' as 'hot, glowing; ardent, intense'. Jesus rebuked the Laodician church for being lukewarm – we need to be 'hot' in our longing for him and his kingdom. God looks for desire, asking us, 'how much do we want his glory to fill our land?' Do we truly care about the condition of our towns, cities and nations? Do we long with intensity for godly transformation – lives set free and healed, and thousands coming to Christ? It is only a Holy Spirit inspired flame within us that will keep us praying in such a manner.

3. To help in equipping believers for harvest

The ministries outlined in Ephesians 4 – apostle, prophet, evangelist, pastor and teacher – which we have already spoken about, are given 'to equip God's people for works of service'. Many in the Church have heard a great amount of teaching, often very good teaching. My concern as one who teaches is how much effect does our teaching have? Does it inform more than bring change or truly equip people to do the work God has called them to? Alongside our more traditional model of teaching we need to meaningfully train, mentor, release and send the people of God. Our best model for this is surely Jesus himself. He called his disciples, spent time with them, had them go round with him as he preached, taught, healed the sick and cast out demons, then encouraged them to do the same, sending them out to do the works of the Kingdom. More and more are recognising this need, but I still think we are not good at this – the long history of emphasis on academic training for ministry still takes its toll. Our aim must be to train God's people in interactive, practical ways so that they can all play their part in the coming harvest.

Not only is there a need for good training in terms of teaching and modelling, many in the Church need to be equipped by being given fresh encouragement. Many church leaders and members have tried so hard and seen so little that they are discouraged, feeling almost defeated. There is a great need for the ministry of encouragement, to instil fresh hope, to inspire to new efforts and to breathe in new breath. We need to encourage the Church to overcome the intimidation of the enemy. When Goliath came against Israel he sought to, and succeeded in, intimidating Saul and his army. Many in the Church can feel intimidated by the volume of sin around us; others have been intimidated from sharing their faith. We need champions like David who will take righteous exception to *'the uncircumcised Philistine who defies the armies of the living God'*, and with the sling of encouragement in hand will fire the stones of God's word that will slay this giant.

4. To see the planting of new churches, and new expressions of Church, alongside the continuing renewal of existing churches

Across our city there is a considerable number of empty church buildings. Grand buildings that were once busy places of worship are now converted into flats, restaurants and dance halls. Others lie empty. It could make for a dismal and discouraging picture of Church decline. Some might look at this scenario and conclude that we need fewer churches. I believe the opposite is true! I believe we need more churches, new churches, totally different types of churches, churches that meet in homes, in halls, even in pubs; churches that meet on Sundays or Mondays; churches that meet late at night or early in the morning.

As we believe for harvest we need to get the nets ready. I love the passage in Luke 5 where the disciples have been fishing all night and exclaim to Jesus, *'we've worked hard all night and caught nothing.'* These were the experts in fishing. They had fished at the best time, but with no fruit. Jesus tells them to *'put out into deep water and let down the nets.'* They do not protest for long, but reply, *'because you say so we will let down our nets.'* Despite some of the natural appearance of how things are, we need to pay heed to the Holy Spirit calling out to us to 'wake up and get ready'.

As we have already said 'one size does not fit all'. If we are to reach whole cities we will need a great variety of churches. That in no way implies that those churches will compromise the truth of the gospel, but it is essential that we present that glorious truth in meaningful ways, and it is equally essential that we build churches that can disciple people from all backgrounds.

We want to encourage these three means for promoting the name of Jesus and extending his Kingdom.

Plant new churches

We do need new church plants for the following reasons.

First, there are areas of our towns and cities where there is no meaningful, evangelistic Christian witness.

Second, with the vast majority of our population not having any living relationship with Christ, there is an enormous harvest field with room for hundreds and thousands more churches across our nation. A new church in an area should not be a threat to existing churches, and its aim must not be to simply 'shuffle the saints', drawing people from other congregations. Though this may have happened, we must not fear the past mistakes, but reach out in this new day to the multitudes in the valley of decision.

Third, we should recognise that often new churches will grow in conversion growth at a higher rate than longer established churches. This is simply a dynamic of life – something new can attract fresh interest, the members are naturally more motivated with the new work and there may be a greater sense of expectation. As churches grow they often then begin to focus more on establishing their people and pastoring the flock.

Fourth, we need a greater variety of churches. I'll expand on this below, but here we should note that it may be smaller churches that will reach proportionately more people, and a planting of many smaller congregations could have much more evangelistic potential than having a smaller number of large congregations.

Fifth, I believe that a new church plant can help renew the existing churches in an area. The new group can help put the evangelistic mandate back on to the agenda, and the presence of another congregation praying for the area can only strengthen the work of the Kingdom of God in that locality.

Create new expressions of Church

While I believe we need to plant new churches, it is important we do not simply replicate what we already have. We need to take the opportunity to do a new thing. The existing styles of Church are not impacting a huge percentage of our nation. Without compromising the truth of our message, we can, and must find ways of being Church that will begin to affect the numbers in our society who are presently unimpressed by the Church. This needs more than simply trying to engage a bit more with our communities. Many churches are seeking to do that more, and that is a good thing, but to really reach the people we need to be much more radical. We want to encourage brave men and women with a call from God to go and plant churches that may not look outwardly a lot like Church as many know it, but will be the right expressions of the life of Christ to the various sectors of our society.

Renew existing churches

While I see the need for new church plants and new expressions of Church, I have great hope for our present churches. Where there is any openness to the Spirit's voice, a few praying people, or a faithful, though maybe nearly worn out leader, then there is great hope. God can break in afresh, quickening the hearts of his people and restoring vision. We need to pray for the Church, rather than criticise it. While we must acknowledge our mistakes and weaknesses, we need to be positive about what God can do rather than bemoan the present situation, or criticise in a negative manner. We are in continual need of renewal by the Holy Spirit, and we need to see the churches in our area encouraged, given a word of hope and purpose, and strengthened once again in the love of Christ.

Conclusion

Our belief and aim at Prayer for the City is to see the Church in our city renewed with the breath of the Spirit of God, restored in its love for Jesus, truly knowing him and making him known, and then reclaiming the city for Christ's glory. We believe for our *'sheep to increase by thousands, by tens of thousands on our hills'* (Psalm 144:13) as the Holy Spirit brings an awakening to our land. We believe for the godly transformation of our city in such a way that the Spirit of Christ affects and impacts every aspect of our city's life.

Notes

1. For more on this subject see Bob Beckett, *Commitment to Conquer* (Chosen Books, 1997).
2. Francis Frangipane, *The House of the Lord* (New Wine Press, 1991), p. 11.
3. Ibid, p. 71.

Chapter 3

Be Impressed with Jesus

Sundays in our church could vary a great deal. Some weeks it was most encouraging as God touched people's lives, other weeks the numbers would be low, sometimes causing us to get quite downhearted about things. But then there were Monday evenings! Now most people look forward to the weekend and often dislike Mondays, but I must say I always looked forward to Monday – and prayer meeting night. These were such refreshing times and I often sensed the Lord speak to me in these meetings – many sermon ideas were birthed in the prayer meeting!

One Monday evening I sensed God was going to say something very important to us. I waited expecting someone to give a word of prophecy or share a vision. Nothing seemed to be coming, and then I sensed the Lord very simply and quickly drop this phrase into my mind: 'Be impressed with Jesus, and he will make his impression on you.' It seemed so simple, yet this was the important word God wanted to give to us. Others there may not even have taken any note when I shared it, but it left a deep imprint in me. Over the months and years I have meditated on this phrase, and believe it is foundational for our lives in Christ and for developing our prayer life.

Many things or people can impress us. We might be impressed by a great achievement or by someone's outstanding ability or his or her incredible mind. We can even be impressed in a negative manner by the scale of crime or evil such that it paralyses us with a sense of hopelessness and fear. The ten spies for the children of Israel were impressed by the giants in the land of Canaan, and would have retreated in fear. Joshua and Caleb, however, were more impressed by the size of their God. Our need is to see Jesus in his glorious risen majesty and be truly impressed by him who sits on the throne.

Magnify the Lord

In Psalm 34:1 David makes this invitation:

> '*O magnify the* LORD *with me,*
> *and let us exalt his name together.*'   (RSV)

To magnify means to increase the apparent size of something using a lens or microscope. So how can we magnify the Lord? How could we possibly increase his size when he is already eternal and immeasurable? Our need is to magnify the Lord in our eyes which is where we have sometimes, maybe often, made him too small. Nothing will actually change about God's 'size' or nature or ability. What will change is our view of him, leading to an increase in our worship of him, and in our faith for what he can do. This is why praise is such a vital part of prayer. As we praise we focus on the majesty and greatness, the love and mercy, the power and compassion of God, so we are stirred to pray for, and believe for, so much more of his divine activity to be displayed on the earth. As we praise the Lord, the enemy is put to flight. Satan cannot operate in an atmosphere of anointed praise and worship where the saints of God are being released in great faith by 'magnifying the Lord'.

Think of a prayer meeting where some believers desire to pray for their area. There are many problems with drugs, violence and family breakdown all around their doorstep. The church is small and struggles financially. Among the believers several are sick or have difficult family situations. Are you feeling depressed yet? They would be if they only focused on all these problems. Instead of focusing there they begin to praise God singing songs and hymns that exalt his name. As they praise, the wonder of God's nature and power is at the forefront of their minds. The Holy Spirit is stirring up their faith in what God can do in their families and in their area. Now they are facing the problems, not denying them, in the light of God's love and power. What a difference it makes when we magnify the Lord.

How do we get impressed with Jesus?

Most of us will have been in encouraging meetings where in praise we have magnified the Lord, and our hearts have been uplifted and our faith has soared. The next morning we can feel very different when faced with the first difficulty of the day. How do we become impressed with Jesus in such a lasting way that he makes his impression on us?

God's goal for your life is that you *'be conformed to the likeness of his Son'* (Romans 8:29). That means he wants to make you more and more like Jesus. He wants the impression, the mark of Jesus' character to be in you. As we press in close to the Lord we put ourselves in a position for him to form more of his likeness in us. As Paul says, *'And we all, with unveiled face, beholding the glory of the Lord, are being changed into his likeness from one degree of glory to another'* (2 Corinthians 3:18, RSV). We need to spend unhurried time 'beholding' the Lord, like David we need to *'gaze upon the beauty of the LORD'* (Psalm 27:4).

In the rest of this chapter we shall take a good look at Jesus letting the Holy Spirit impress us with his beauty.

Impressed with his life

Many people have been, and many still are, impressed with the life of Jesus Christ. This includes those who reject the Church and the Christian faith. Mahatma Ghandi based practices in his life on the example and teaching of Jesus even though he rejected the Christian faith. Many people say that they admire the life of Jesus, though they are not always impressed with his followers. Some will speak of Jesus as the greatest teacher even though they do not put their faith in him as Lord and Saviour. As believers we need to allow ourselves to be so impressed with Jesus that he does make his impression on us.

Let us take a brief look at aspects of the life of the most impressive man to walk the earth.

His teaching

Jesus did not teach like the teachers of the law in his day, but taught with authority (Mark 1:27). And his teaching had such authority that it did not just inform and educate people, but changed their lives. His teaching with such authority caused demons to manifest and be cast out. He did not have to quote from other teachers, as was the practice of the day, but spoke from the Scriptures, bringing divine interpretation and fresh revelation from the Father.

His teaching was profound and not always understood by his disciples, yet had a simplicity about, *'do to others what you would have them do to you'* (Matthew 7:14). His teaching was prophetic and practical, challenging and changing people. He cut to the motives of the heart, yet lifted up the needy.

His miraculous works

Some theologians have tried to explain away the miracles as myths, attempting to accommodate a scientific worldview. This has not only dishonoured the truth of God's Word, but has also been unhelpful in promoting the gospel. Indeed it is often in nations where the miraculous works of God are most widely acknowledged that there is the greatest growth in the Church. We deny the gospel when we deny the miracles of Jesus. Instead we should look at his miraculous works and see in them the wonder of God's love, grace and power. The wonder of blind eyes being opened, the lame walking, the deaf hearing, withered hands being restored, and the dead being raised. We see in Jesus miraculous works, the Kingdom of God breaking in bringing hope, healing and new life.

His servant heart

> *'For even the Son of Man did not come to be served, but to serve . . .'*   (Mark 10:45)

Jesus moved in great power and authority. He has been the most influential person ever to live on earth, yet he showed such a beautiful servant attitude in his life. His humble service is truly outstanding, and he always encouraged that same humility and serving attitude among his followers, a point that continuously needs to be well noted in the Church wherever there is any hint of personal power and prestige.

His attitude of compassion

As Jesus moved about among the people, encountering much suffering and need, we are impressed by his compassion (Matthew 9:36). He had great compassion – literally 'moved in his guts' – for lepers who had been made outcasts, for widows and those in grief, and for the crowds of needy and oppressed people. Jesus felt deeply for people, not a mere sympathetic thought, and his words and actions not only proved his compassion, but also showed he had the power to bring about transformation.

His integrity

We cannot fail to be impressed by the integrity of Jesus. Even his opponents acknowledged his integrity, and that he was not swayed by men's opinions (Matthew 22:16).

Jesus never sought popularity, and never changed his opinions or words in order to please people.

His prayer life

We will look at his practice of prayer more fully in chapter 7, but again we cannot but be impressed by his relationship to the Father and his life of prayer.

Impressed with his death

Paul says,

> *'Very rarely 'will anyone die for a righteous man ... But God demonstrates his own love for us in this: While we were still sinners, Christ died for us.'*   (Romans 5:7–8)

Everything about the way Jesus died is impressive. He laid down his life voluntarily of his own accord (John 10:18); he died with great courage, and with concern, not for himself, but for others. He could have called down angels to release him, but willingly submitted himself to the taunts of his opponents (Mark 15:29–32). His dying words were for forgiveness for those who hung him to the cruel cross. We are impressed by the sacrificial love of our glorious Saviour.

I remember a scene from a film where a wounded prisoner of war is sitting in an enemy village. His injuries make any escape impossible and he is left relatively unattended. A group of village children nearby to him pick up a hand grenade and start to play with it as if it were a ball. One pulls out the pin. The wounded soldier, seeing this, summons enough strength to leap forward, catching the grenade, and as he dives out of the way the grenade goes off killing him. The children look on with stunned faces at the death of an enemy soldier who laid down his life to save them. It would have been highly unlikely that this wounded man would have done anything this noble for the armed, adult enemy soldiers.

Jesus died for the human race: for those who had rejected and despised him, for all who have rebelled against him. He not only died for us but also took our sin upon himself.

Not only was the manner in which he laid down his life so impressive, so also is the power of his death. This death was not defeat, but victory. It is the turning point for all mankind, for all history, as the blood of the sinless One is shed for the forgiveness of all our sins. It is the death that the evil one has no answer to, for it is the death that defeated him, and signals his final destruction. Against the death of Christ Satan can bring no accusation. How we need to 'survey the wondrous cross' over and over, letting its impact touch us afresh.

Impressed with his resurrection

Paul writes emphatically to the Corinthians, *'Death has been swallowed up in victory'* (1 Corinthians 15:54). While it is right to focus much on the amazing love and sacrificial death of Christ, we must likewise focus on his glorious resurrection. What transformed the frightened disciples into bold witnesses was their absolute conviction and certainty that Jesus had risen, such that they were willing to die for him. This conviction, along with the infilling of the Holy Spirit, enabled these men to *'testify to the resurrection of the Lord Jesus with great power'* (see Acts 4:33).

We see in Jesus the Risen One who has conquered our final enemy of death, and breaks the power of fear over our lives. Death could not keep its hold on the sinless Son of God; it had no right over him. He is risen, living forever, the eternal King of kings.

Jesus raised the dead during his ministry on earth but each one he raised died again, though maybe many years later. Jesus was raised immortal having totally vanquished death. He lives for all eternity as the King of Glory.

Impressed with his eternal position

He has risen and is now exalted to the highest place, having been given the name above every name (Philippians 2:9). He is now seated *'far above all rule and authority, power and dominion, and every title that can be given, not only in the present age but also in the one to come'* (see Ephesians 1:20–23). Revelation chapter 5 paints the glorious picture of the 'risen, conquering Son'. We see the contrast of the Lamb who is a Lion. The One who looks as if he has been slain is also he who has triumphed. So we worship the Lamb upon the throne declaring with all heaven's hosts,

'Worthy is the Lamb, who was slain,
to receive power and wealth and wisdom and strength
and honour and glory and praise ...
    for ever and ever!' (Revelation 5:12–13)

There is so much about Jesus that is truly impressive. Our life could be devoted to gazing upon him and we would continually see fresh wonders about him. The various aspects of his Person all come together to form what we call the 'beauty of the Lord'.

Impressed with his beauty

My dictionary defines beauty this way: 'combination of qualities, as shape, proportion, colour ... that delights the sight; combined qualities delighting the other senses, the moral sense, the intellect'. The beauty of a garden would usually be found in the variety and combination of the colours and scents of the flowers. So the beauty of Jesus is found in the wonderful and unique combination of his attributes. The desire of David's heart was this:

'One thing I ask of the LORD,
    this is what I seek:
That I may dwell in the house of the LORD,
    all the days of my life,
to gaze upon the beauty of the LORD
    and to seek him in his temple.' (Psalm 27:4)

Jesus is altogether lovely, our Beautiful Saviour, and we will find that time spent gazing upon his beauty is time well spent. So often in our frenetic lives we may glance his way. If we are to be impressed with him, and find his impression marked in our lives and on our characters, then we must find the time to gaze in awe on the Glorious Son of God.

What will this lead to?

Initially such gazing or beholding of the Lord in his beauty will lead to worship welling up inside us and overflowing in praise and thanksgiving. In the Old Testament we find this wonderful promise:

> *'Your eyes will see the king in his beauty,*
> *and view a land that stretches afar.'* (Isaiah 33:17)

God's promise is that we will see him in his beauty – we need to give ourselves to look for him and gaze upon him. Following that is the promise that we will *'view a land that stretches afar'*. This is a spacious place, so important to the Israelites in their inheritance of the land. It is a place like Isaac found (Genesis 26) when he kept digging wells, finally getting away from all the disputes and quarrelling, he names the well 'Rehoboth' meaning room, a spacious place, and he says *'we will flourish in the land'*.

When we get a true view of Jesus, when we focus and centre our lives on him, when we are far, far more impressed with him than with anyone or anything else, then we will move into that spacious place. Then the wrongly restrictive boundaries that have been put around us by our unbelief, other people's negative opinions, or demonic activity, will be blown away and we will move into the greater fullness of God's purpose for our lives within the boundaries that he has set for us in pleasant places (Psalm 16:6).

When we left the pastoral ministry in 1999 we had to leave the church's house and move into rented accommodation. While three house moves inside two years have proved to be quite an upheaval, we had the pleasure of renting a cottage on a farm just outside the city. Fields and moorland, with a spectacular view of Glasgow, surrounded us. The concept of God giving us a spacious place in the Spirit from which to grow and flourish in ministry was strong within us, and so we just had to name this house 'Rehoboth'. In a physical way it represented what we felt God was saying about how our lives were to be in Christ. We got a friend to carve a wooden sign and put it on the door post. If nothing else it got visitors and the postman asking questions.

Conclusion

God's purpose for our lives is to make us into the likeness of Jesus. In all that he does, and all that he allows to happen in our lives, he is always looking to form more of his Son's character in us. That is why every circumstance can work for our good, for the highest good is becoming more like him. In victory or defeat, in success or failure, in health or sickness, in joy or grief – in all situations God can work more of his good and pleasing purpose in us. We co-operate with this work when we turn our eyes, our gaze on Jesus, and being impressed with him, he is making his impression on us.

SECTION 2

Overcoming Obstacles

Introduction

Having our minds and hearts focused on Jesus, our Great High Priest, we can enter more effectively into the task of intercessory prayer. In this section (chapters 4–6) we will look at three accounts from the gospels where a parent came in persevering prayer to Jesus on behalf of one of their children. In each of these cases we will examine the obstacles that they came up against and how those obstacles were overcome.

We will observe from these chapters, as we do from other Scriptures and lessons of history, that persevering in prayer is vital. In fact persevering is one of the best assets in all Christian ministry and service. I saw this in a very simple situation one day.

I had taken some time out one beautiful summer's day to go away and seek the Lord in prayer. I dropped my family off at the coast and took a road inland up into the hills. The sun was shining brilliantly and the scenery all around was magnificent. However, as I drove along this narrow road there appeared to be no place to stop. There was another car in front of me, and after quite some distance they finally stopped and turned at a farmyard entrance and went back. I felt I should maybe do likewise, but sensed the Lord prompt me to keep going round one more corner. As I drove round the next bend in the road the most stunning view of the hills, a river and a small loch opened up before me, and overlooking this scene was a lay-by for parking. Like the car that was in front of me we can stop just short of the breakthrough or answer to prayer. It can be hard to keep going at times. We feel like children on a long journey who keep asking how much further, with the parents repeatedly replying, 'just a little bit more'. But often in prayer and ministry we do just have to press on that little bit more.

Chapter 4

Overcoming Obstacles 1:
A Determined Mother

The Canaanite woman
(Matthew 15:21–28; Mark 7:24–30)

There are many determined mothers in the world. Sometimes that is a marvellous attribute in mothers wanting the best for their children, other times it is not so good, if the determination is for the mother to get her way for her children. In this passage we discover a determined mother – and in the very best way.

This Canaanite (or Syro-Phoenician) woman came to Jesus out of deep concern for her daughter. Most translations say that her daughter was demon-possessed though the extremity of that term is neither accurate nor helpful. The Greek word is better rendered 'demonised' or 'affected by a demon'. To translate this word as 'possession' is to suggest her life was totally taken over and controlled by demonic forces, which is highly unlikely. The term also gives the impression that very few today would be affected in such a manner. I believe the truth is that many people today are affected by demons and we do them no service by denying this. Instead we need to acknowledge this situation and bring the truth and authority of Jesus name to those who are oppressed and set them free.

Like others in the gospel accounts this woman saw and seized the opportunity. Jesus had come to her area and she was not going to let this chance pass her by. Similarly we can read of Bartimaeus, the blind beggar, who, when he heard it was Jesus passing through his town, cried out and would not be put off by anyone (see Mark 10:46–52). In this case Jesus had withdrawn to this area to get some rest and did not want anyone knowing he was there. Such was this mother's determination and desperation that she came to Jesus as soon as she heard about his presence (Mark 7:25). Her cry was the only cry we can really make to the Lord, that is, 'have mercy on me'. None of us deserve God's favour, nor can we claim a right to it because we have worked hard for him. We have no bargaining power with the King of Glory, though people sometimes try that tack. How many have prayed saying to God, 'if you will only answer this need then I will do this for you'. Such promises to be a better Christian or go to church every Sunday are not often kept once the crisis has passed.

The wonderful truth about mercy and grace is that we do not need to bargain or earn. He does not treat us as our sins deserve, but instead is full of compassion and mercy towards us. God looks for the humble and dependent, yet determined heart's cry, and that is what this mother brings to his ears. In this fascinating passage we observe the unfolding of a surprising discourse between Jesus, his disciples and this woman, a discourse that tested her determination to the limit.

We will examine each of three obstacles this Canaanite woman had to overcome as she persevered in intercession for her suffering daughter.

Obstacle 1: No response (Matthew 15:23)

'Jesus did not answer a word.' This seems so unlike him, the one who reached out and touched lepers to whom nobody else would go near, the one who was filled with compassion for the needs of the people. Surely she had gone to Jesus because his reputation had spread, a reputation for having the power to heal and a concern for the oppressed. How must she have felt at this ignoring of her plea?

There is something in all of us that does not like to be ignored, and one of our greatest fears is the fear of being rejected. Think of a young man wanting to ask an attractive girl out on a date. He hesitates and seeks to work up the courage because he is afraid she might say no. In fact it might be worse if she simply turned away and ignored him altogether.

While we may know that God loves us and cares about us, and have experienced his answers to prayers, we can still find times when we call out to him and no answer or response appears to come. We can feel he has ignored us and wonder if he is listening. We find such cries in the Psalms: *'How long?'* (6:3); *'Why, O Lord, do you stand far off?'* (10:1) and several others of a similar note (e.g. 13:1; 22:1–2).

The 'silence' of God

I believe God speaks to his children, rescues and delivers us, and answers prayer. The greater our expectancy of God doing these things the greater our perplexity can be when he appears silent or inactive. So why does God appear to be silent at times? Let me suggest a few thoughts:

1. Divine delays

Wesley Duewel says, 'There is often great mystery concerning the time span required in prevailing prayer. The secret of prevailing prayer is simply to pray until the answer comes.'[1] It is apparent that God has certain times for things and that we sometimes have to wait. Abraham had a long wait for the promised son, Isaac. David had to wait many years from Samuel's prophecy and anointing for him to be king until that was fulfilled. It is so important to discern whether we must press in now for the answer, or keep praying with a patience that knows God will answer in his time. This way we do not fall into the trap of stopping praying under the excuse of 'it's maybe not God's time'.

2. Drawing out desire

As I have said earlier, God looks for desire in our hearts, and may delay in order to test that desire. He is looking to see how much we really care, and how much we truly long for his answers and his Kingdom to come.

A wise parent does not simply grant every request of their children immediately. If they ask for a computer, the parent will often test how much they really desire and will make use of this product by making them wait and having to ask over and over again.

We might also think of a children's Christmas party waiting for Santa to arrive. The youngsters have to sing 'Jingle bells' to get Santa to come in. They are then encouraged to sing it louder and louder if they really want the bearer of their toys to arrive.

3. Deal with debts

Of course it may be that we have got some sin issues to clear up. Have we something to confess? Have we someone to forgive? There are blocks that we can erect that shut out the response of God. The words of Jesus make this very clear (see Matthew 5:23, 24; 6:14–15; Mark 11:24–25).

There may be many other reasons in the divine mystery – sometimes God may not answer our small request as he wants to give us much more than we ask or imagine.

Commentators offer some possible explanations of why Jesus did not answer this woman. They ask such questions as whether he was figuring out if he should help her or not as she was not of the people of Israel. Whatever the reason in this case, and whatever the reason for you and I experiencing this 'silent response' at times, what is important is that we learn from this woman's response and how she overcame this obstacle. We shall look at her responses after we examine the other two obstacles she encountered.

Obstacle 2: The disciples wanted to send her away
(Matthew 15:23)

This is not the only time that the disciples tried to send away those seeking the Lord's touch (e.g. Mark 10:13). It may well be that these men meant well and were trying to protect Jesus from people bothering him. Maybe they wanted to be alone with Jesus, and encouraged by his lack of response to the woman, they press home the point for a time of peace and quiet. Again we need not over concern ourselves with these speculations, but look at how we encounter this obstacle.

I have found that over the twenty plus years that I have been a committed Christian I have been very enthusiastic at times about the Lord and his Kingdom. Some of that enthusiasm may have been rather immature or self-motivated, but the Spirit of God has inspired much of it. I have found many believers who have encouraged my enthusiasm, some wise people who have redirected it a little, but also found some who have sought to dampen it down. It may be that you have had something of your enthusiasm to see God move in power dampened by those who seem mature, but are maybe more afraid of such enthusiasm and the changes it might set in motion through prayer and action. It may be that you have had great faith in prayer to pray some really big prayers, but have felt rebuked by those of a different disposition.

This Canaanite mother must have felt rebuked and discouraged by those close to Jesus. Hannah was similarly rebuked by Eli who did not understand her passionate pleas before God, and suspected she was drunk (1 Samuel 1:12–14).

Obstacle 3: Outside the boundary of God's activity
(Matthew 15:24, 26)

The third obstacle that this determined mother came up against is that when Jesus finally spoke to her his words were far from encouraging, suggesting that she was outside the sphere of his ministry and God's activity. Not only so, but he also used quite insulting language in describing her status.

We can feel the same at times. Stories of great moves of God in other parts of the earth, such as we have watched on the *Transformations* videos, can encourage us, adding fuel to our prayers and building our faith. However, they can also leave us wondering why other places appear to receive God's favour and we do not. We can be truly pleased for someone we hear testifying how they prayed for their son for years and now he has come to the Lord, yet at the same time wonder why the one we are praying for still seems to be 'in a far off land'. We hear of others being healed and praise the Lord for it, but maybe we are still sick, even with the same condition. We maybe try and repress the questioning, but our heart is crying out, 'what about me, Lord?' and 'what about my city or nation?'

After his resurrection Jesus sent the disciples into all the earth, to all peoples. God's boundary does reach to every one of us, and to our towns, cities and nations. His grace is sufficient and his love knows no bounds. However, prayer can be puzzling.

This mother approached Jesus in great hope, but received a puzzling response. She met with some serious hurdles in her quest to get healing and deliverance for her daughter. But she remained undaunted; she was one determined lady.

Let us now examine her responses and see what we can learn from them.

This woman's responses

1. Continued to ask in an attitude of worship
(Matthew 15:25)

The woman knelt before Jesus in a position of worship before him, and continued her plea for help. As we persevere in prayer it is vitally important to keep doing so in an attitude of worship. Especially in the dry and difficult times, when it seems as if God is not answering, we must continue to humbly worship because of who he is. It is so much easier to praise the Lord when the answers are coming and good things are happening all around. The key test of our faith is whether we can praise him when things are tough.

As we worship we keep our hearts turned towards God in a way that keeps anger and bitterness at bay. It is not so much the trials or wounds that come our way that affect us, but how we respond to those circumstances that will have the lasting effect on our lives and our character.

2. Did not take offence but pressed in

The Canaanite woman did not dispute her status or argue for her right to be heard. She did not question Jesus' remarks or demand fairer treatment. She just wanted her daughter healed.

How easily some people can take offence and allow this to destroy relationships. Even if someone else gives offence, you do not have to take it! Paul asks, *'Why not rather be wronged?'* (1 Corinthians 6:7). Somewhere along the line of our lives many of us have picked up the idea that we have rights. Our society speaks of the right to free speech, the right to remain silent, the right to work, the right to benefits and so on. We feel we have the right to our own opinion – even if it's not a very good one! We feel we have the right to take offence. When we come to Christ and make him Lord we surrender any rights we thought we had. He has right of way in our lives now, and hopefully we trust him to have his way. If we still think we have some right in God's sight, then we will be offended by him at times, and in danger of this severely damaging our relationship with him. However, if we follow the example of this woman we will come to the Lord on the ground of his mercy alone. The right we do have in Christ is the right to come to the throne of grace at any time. We need to come to that holy place with unoffended hearts, pressing in for the grace and mercy we need.

3. Asked even for a crumb (Matthew 15:27)

Again we see that the Canaanite took no offence at being referred to as a dog, but used the very illustration to appeal for just a crumb. She realised that even a 'crumb' of Jesus' power would set her daughter free. Such is the awesome power and authority of our Lord that just a drop of his Spirit's power can transform lives. Yet God wants to give us so much more. He wants to give us 'the whole loaf' that will transform whole cities and nations.

Jesus responds
'Woman, you have great faith! Your request is granted.'
(Matthew 15:28)

The perseverance of this determined mother paid off. In her undeterred asking Jesus saw *'great faith'* and her daughter was set free and healed.

Conclusion

The power of the persevering prayers of many a parent and grandparent have been a means of many mighty works of God in the lives of those for whom they prayed. I think I am one of the answers. For the many parents, and others, who are still crying out for someone or some breakthrough, thinking God has not heard, or thinking of giving up, then look at the example of this Canaanite woman and press in regardless of all else, looking to the mercy of our loving Father in heaven.

Note
1. Wesley Duewel, *Mighty Prevailing Prayer* (Zondervan, 1990), p. 17.

Chapter 5

Overcoming Obstacles 2:
A Desperate Father

Jairus (Mark 5:21–24, 35–43; Luke 8:40–56)

Reading from Mark 4:35–5:43 we discover a tremendous catalogue of the miraculous works of Jesus, displaying his unquestionable authority and demonstrating the Kingdom rule of God. First of all we observe Jesus' authority over the forces of nature as he calms the storm on the lake. Crossing to the other side of the lake we see his authority over the demonic powers as he sets free a man so demonised that he had been bound in chains. From there we come to our passage where we find Jesus healing an incurably sick woman, hence displaying his authority over disease, and finally raising a dead girl, thus demonstrating that ultimate authority over the power of death. Demons, disease, death and the forces of nature must all submit to the authoritative word of the Son of God.

Jairus, a religious man and ruler in the synagogue, was in a desperate situation. His little girl, just twelve years of age, was dying. Literally she was at the end. Jairus only had one hope – the man who was demonstrating the authority of God over all things.

> *'Then one of the synagogue rulers, named Jairus, came there. Seeing Jesus, he fell at his feet and pleaded earnestly with him,*

"My little daughter is dying. Please come and put your hands on her so that she will be healed and live." So Jesus went with him.'
(Mark 5:22–24a)

What do we notice about Jairus?

- **He was a ruler in the synagogue**. Unlike the Canaanite woman in chapter 4, Jairus was one of the sheep of Israel. In fact he was no doubt a very religious and devout man.
- **Jairus sees Jesus**. He catches sight of the One he was looking for. It is similarly vital for us to 'see Jesus' when we come to intercessory prayer. When we have great needs and are praying for miracles we need to have a sight of Jesus in his power and authority, that we might be filled with faith as we look to him.
- **He falls at Jesus feet**. Despite being a leader in the synagogue he shows no sign that he thinks he deserves anything, but throws himself humbly at the feet of Jesus.
- **He pleads earnestly**. He is a desperate man. He loves his daughter, and is distraught at her plight. His prayer is truly a fervent one. It often takes desperate circumstances to drive us to this sort of fervency in prayer, though I believe we need to become so desperate for God's Kingdom to come, and his will to be done, thus putting such fervency into our praying.
- **He has great faith**. He is desperate, but also has much faith, believing that if Jesus lays his hands on the girl then she will live. Sometimes people may pray out of desperation, but at the same time their hearts are full of fear, not really believing that God will answer and intervene. But humility, desperation and faith make up a potent combination.

Jairus' heart would now be filling with a sense of real hope – Jesus is coming with him. His heartbeat pounds with anticipation, but also anxiety, as he wonders if they will get to his daughter in time. There is a large crowd all around, but Jairus has got Jesus' attention and he is going to his house. His mind is on his precious little girl back home, and he is almost oblivious to the noise and bustle of the crowd. Then Jesus stops. He turns around and asks a seemingly crazy question, *'who touched me?'* The crowd is pressing against him, but Jesus knows someone has reached out in faith and *'power had gone out from him.'* Jesus waits for the person to respond – a woman who had been subject to bleeding for twelve years – the length of Jairus' daughter's life. He maybe waited just a few moments, but it must have seemed agonisingly long to Jairus. Would his heart not be questioning the importance of this healing when his daughter is at the point of death?

Jesus finds the woman and speaks words of healing and peace to her, bringing restoration to a previously unclean person. But as Jesus is speaking these very words of comfort to this woman, servants from Jairus' house arrive bringing the news that Jairus had been dreading.

So he comes to his first major obstacle.

Obstacle 4: The situation gets worse

His daughter had been dying, but at least there was hope. Now she is dead. It is over. I have prayed for a number of terminally ill people, and prayed with some faith and hope that they might be healed. I have also had to conduct a number of their funerals. There is a time to die, and a time to deal with that and bring comfort to those who grieve. The lesson that I believe we have to learn here is that when we pray things can start to get worse, but we must not give up because of that.

When Moses confronted Pharaoh (Exodus 5:22–23) things got a lot worse for the Israelites. Moses began to question what God was up to. When we begin to pray seriously for our community, that people will be saved, healed and set free from the power of darkness, then we will move into a new level of warfare and come under some strong testing. For example, when we press in with deliverance prayer the enemy may press in hard against us. His purpose is to put us off. He cannot destroy us – he needs God's permission to come against us – and God may allow that in order to test our commitment. I have found it helpful when the enemy attacks on such occasions to declare aloud that the more he attacks the more I will teach on and expose his works, and press in to pray for more deliverance of those in his captivity.

So when we pray earnestly for breakthroughs for people, our churches and our communities, we can find that the following gives the appearance that things are getting worse.

1. Sudden problems and troubles flare up in our own lives or the lives of those close to us

We have found this to happen on many occasions over the years, especially when we have started some new work, been involved in deliverance prayer ministry, or taken new steps for citywide unity.

The key for us is to not fear these 'attacks', but to see what the enemy is trying to do, namely to stop us from praying or doing what we are doing. Our adversary seeks to intimidate us and cause us to shrink back. He will do this by trying to give us the impression that if we pursue our present course things will get very difficult and even nasty. He also seeks to intimidate by accusing us of past failures and faults. My past mistakes are numerous, but I thank the Lord they are covered in the blood, and hopefully some lessons have been learnt. What the enemy sends against us can in fact be used to strengthen us and cause us to lean more on the Lord.

However, we must not fall into the trap of viewing every little thing that goes wrong as being the enemy attacking us. Discovering you have a flat tyre on the way to a prayer meeting may simply be that you ran over a nail. Do not glorify the evil one by crediting him with things he has not done. We need to keep a balanced outlook, being aware of Satan's schemes but not seeing demons behind every little mishap.

2. The person or situation that we are interceding about appears to get worse

Especially when we begin to pray about areas of bondage and enemy strongholds we can feel like we are disturbing a hornet's nest. I suppose we are! Demonic powers will work away quietly, slowly destroying the goodness of life that God has given. When the spotlight is shone upon them they will flare up. They do not want to be exposed, but once they are, they will react strongly.

In other situations too there can be an initial deterioration for various reasons, including the Lord allowing our resolve to be tested, or bringing the person we are interceding for to rock bottom where they depend totally on God and truly desire his salvation with all their heart.

3. We pray concerning the presenting problems or symptoms, and the Holy Spirit begins to strip away to reveal the root issue

Having had to move house three times in a short space of time we have seen quite a bit of change. Recently we had building work done and a considerable amount of redecoration. Now I do not take a lot of notice of the colour or design of our wallpaper and therefore do not notice if it is in need of redecoration. Helen makes these decisions; I just hand over the money, and pick up the rolls of wallpaper and tins of paint from the store. Once we start stripping the walls it looks a real mess. I sometimes think we should not have started but just have left it alone. However, once all the work is completed even I notice the difference and have to acknowledge it was worthwhile.

Similarly when we pray for an individual or a given situation we begin to focus on the outward symptoms, but soon find other issues are uncovered as our praying moves the Holy Spirit to strip away the outward coverings and defences. In prayer ministry we might pray with someone whose presenting problem is recurring headaches. As we begin to pray it soon becomes apparent that something else is wrong, and we realise we are in for a long session, and maybe a few more to follow. We need to persevere in these situations, refusing to stop short. The simple truth is this: often things will get worse before they get better.

The problem occurs with the above when we draw our conclusions from the deteriorating circumstances rather than God's Word. Like the story told of a church meeting in very difficult circumstances. The leader opened the meeting in prayer, declaring the truths of God's character, his power and might, and that nothing was impossible to the Lord. He then addressed the church members with his opening statement, 'the situation in this church is quite hopeless.'

Obstacle 5: Negative voices – 'Why bother?'

The servants from Jairus' house, like the gentleman above, have concluded that the situation is now hopeless. The little girl has now died so there is no point in bothering or troubling Jesus any longer. On the face of it they might appear to be quite right. However, 'the teacher' that Jairus is bothering is the Anointed One, who has just calmed a storm, cast out a legion of demons and healed a woman of an infirmity that had plagued her for twelve years. Besides, he encourages us to bother him, like the man in the parable he told who goes to his neighbour's door at midnight and hammers until he is answered and receives what he needs (Luke 11:5–13).

There is no lack of negative voices around us. You do not have to go far on any given day to find someone complaining or bemoaning the state of things. They may have some justification too, for there is a fair amount of evidence all around us of what is wrong in our world and in our lives. Watching the news on almost any day we will be bombarded with stories of tragedy and atrocity. We can easily find reasons to be glum, negative and pessimistic. Thankfully there are positive voices, hopeful signs, and above all the promises of God.

As we pray about many of the ills and wrongs in our city or in the world, it would be quite possible to be overwhelmed by the scale of the problems and evils. We could ask ourselves what the point is of all this effort.

There are enough sceptics around to pour doubt on our prayerful hopes for revival and a great move of God's Spirit. There are plenty of rational voices that would declare that the change we long and pray for is not likely to happen. They have looked at the evidence and concluded there is little or no hope. There are some people in our world that will go even further and ridicule our efforts.

Obstacle 6: Mocking laughter

This is exactly what Jesus encountered when he got to Jairus' house. The woman with the issue of blood now healed and sorted out, the negative voices ignored, Jesus and Jairus, along with Peter, James and John, finally get to the house where the little girl lies. They are greeted by the customary commotion of those wailing – not so much of the genuinely grieving family members, but the hired mourners (a practice of the day to help the grieving process). Unlike in our modern western culture, where death is so feared that we often attempt to hide it in a way that can really hinder the healthy grieving of bereaved people, the people in this situation encouraged the expression of loud emotions.

Jesus tells them that the girl is not dead, but asleep. They laugh at him, knowing she is dead, and revealing the insincerity of their loud wails. Undeterred Jesus takes command of the situation and raises the little girl from the dead.

Being laughed at is a most sought after experience, and yet something to be avoided at almost any cost. To come out with amusing and witty remarks, giving people a laugh, tends to make us feel good about ourselves and popular with others. On the other hand to be laughed at because of something stupid that we have said or done is normally considered embarrassing and leaves us feeling like we want the ground to open up and swallow us.

It is not so bad if we make a bit of a fool of ourselves by accident. As long as we do not take ourselves too seriously we can usually laugh off such occasions. The real problem comes when we are being absolutely serious about something and people respond by laughing at us in a mocking manner. It is this fear that has hindered many sincere Christians from sharing their faith with others. This fear has also caused many of us not to say anything in situations where we have had a valid contribution to make, but it seemed safer to be silent and not risk any ridicule.

We may have the faith to pray for some miracle but can be hindered by the fear of looking foolish if we speak or pray it out and nothing happens, or fear that more sceptical minds will put us down. One of the schemes of the evil one is to attempt to silence us – to silence our testimony, to silence the prophetic voice, and to silence bold prayers of faith. Paul says to the Corinthians, quoting Psalm 116, *'I believed, therefore I have spoken'* (2 Corinthians 4:13).

Having outlined and examined these obstacles that were encountered both by Jairus and by Jesus in this passage, let us now see how they were overcome.

The responses

Jairus does not make much response himself to these discouraging factors, but goes along with the responses of Jesus.

1. *Don't be afraid, just believe*

This could sound naive, but if it takes a miracle to heal the girl, it also takes a miracle to raise her from the dead. The God who created all things can do either. Jesus seeks to reassure Jairus that although the situation appears to have worsened in a quite critical way, he need not fear.

We should not fall to the fear of any worsening situation, but believe in the promise that led us to pray in the first place. Remember, the enemy attempts to cause us to fear through intimidation and accusation. On the other hand the greeting of God and his angelic messengers to people, and Jesus himself to his disciples, was very often 'do not fear'.

Once we were called to see a young woman whose family was associated with our church. She was 23 weeks pregnant and serious problems had developed, so much so that the doctors told her she would either have to have an abortion or have the baby by caesarean operation. Thankfully she chose to have the baby, and the little one was born weighing a minute one pound and one ounce. There seemed little likelihood of her survival, or that if she did survive then some serious problems were expected. The family and our church went to prayer. We persevered and persevered, though at times there were scares. We believed that God had given this little girl life. After three-and-a-half months she was released from hospital, being featured in national newspapers and on national television, and has grown to be a healthy little girl.

2. Listen to God's words, not the apparently rational voices of other people

Jesus simply ignored what the messengers said. It was not relevant. We do not look at the challenges, problems and needs of life from a worldly point of view, but from the vantage point of faith in God. While we are hoping to see positive changes in the lives of those we pray for, or in our church or our community, we are not to be put off or discouraged by setbacks. God is still Almighty, and the harder the situation, or the greater the need, then the better the opportunity for God to reveal his grace and power.

In 1994 I believed God spoke to me one night saying that we as a local church had cursed ourselves as a 'poor church'. I shared this with my elders who confirmed that people had said such things over the years, and we recognised this was a word from God. We called the church together, shared this with them, repented and broke the curse, and then in faith received the blessing of God. We felt we then had to take a step of faith in line with the prayers we had made. At that time we received a generous grant each year from the Baptist Union that covered about 40% of my stipend. However, we believed God had spoken and the right action for us to take was to thank the Union for all its support, but to now stop receiving the grant aid. After all we were no longer a poor church. Now we did not have any accountants in the church, but if we had they might have been pulling their hair out. The figures would not add up, and it was my pay that was on the line! Rational voices might have suggested we lower the grant a little and see how things go. But in this case God had clearly spoken to us. And so it proved that over the coming months we not only saw an increase in income, that enabled us to meet all our expenses, but we were able to employ a second worker for a period of time. Considering the size and location of our church this was all quite remarkable.

It is very important how we listen and who we listen to, as Jesus said, *'consider carefully how you listen'* (Luke 8:18). We do need to listen to the wise advice of others, including, for example, doctors in cases of medical sickness. However, our faith to pray must not be quenched even by the wise, but limited understanding of others.

3. Put out the mocking, sceptical ones

Jesus deliberately only took his three 'inner circle' disciples with him. He then takes them and the girl's parents into the room, putting out all others, especially the mockers.

When we are praying, whether interceding from a distance or praying with a person who is present, it is important to be surrounded by those who have faith for God to answer our prayers. We may have to actively distance ourselves from those who are sceptical and mocking. However, remember that sometimes those who are not Christians can have more expectancy that God will answer our prayers than some Christians may have. Also there is a big difference between genuine doubts, and stubborn unbelief or a cynical attitude. Psalm 1 exhorts us to *'not walk in the counsel of the wicked or stand in the way of sinners or sit in the seat of mockers'* (Psalm 1:1).

I am quite happy to have those who are maybe not yet Christians attend prayer meetings, in fact I think it can be very good for them, but I do find it a hindrance to prayer when you are battling against a mocking or over sceptical attitude.

Conclusion

With the obstacles brushed aside, and with faith triumphing over fear, Jesus gently, yet with authority, brings the girl back to life.

There are many today, and increasingly so among the young, where the life is being taken from them. The effects of the ills that plague our society – drugs, family breakdown, abuse, hopelessness and fear – and the oppressing, life-stifling demonic power that is released through many of these things, weigh heavily upon many people around us.

As intercessors before the throne of grace, we need to cry out in faith, not fear; we need to hear God's heart and word for the people of our communities, and not be pulled down by the negative, sceptical sounds. We need to call to the Author of Life to raise up the dying ones, to breathe new life into them by his Spirit, so that, as in Jairus' house, so in our land, people might be completely astonished at the wonderful works of our Saviour.

Chapter 6

Overcoming Obstacles 3:
A Doubting Father

The father of a demonised boy
(Mark 9:14–29; Luke 9:37–45)

So far we have come across six obstacles to persevering in prayer from the passages we looked at in the previous two chapters. In this chapter we shall examine two more that could have caused this father to stop short, two obstacles that we can face and need to learn to overcome.

Setting the scene
Jesus and his three closest disciples – Peter, James and John – have been on the mountaintop where the disciples have witnessed incredible phenomena (Mark 9:2–13). Jesus' appearance was transformed before their eyes, and Elijah and Moses appeared speaking with the Lord. The Father's voice sounds forth from a cloud of glory, stating, *'This is my Son, whom I love. Listen to him!'* What an amazing experience! What moments of glory appearing on earth! The disciples were bewildered, frightened and in awe. Jesus receives a powerful affirmation of the Father's love and approval, and the disciples are left in no doubt that their Master is the one to be listened to.

As we leave the glory of the mountaintop we look at the scene in the valley below. A man has brought his son to the

66

remaining disciples and sought their help to drive out the demon that is ruining his boy's life. The disciples try to cast out the demon but with no success, and no doubt considerable commotion. A crowd has gathered, and the teachers of the law see the failure of the disciples and engage in a heated argument with them, a picture contrasting greatly from the one on the mountain.

On the mountain we see the manifest Presence of God; in the valley there is the manifestation of the demonic. On the mountain the voice of God is heard speaking precisely, clearly and powerfully; in the valley there is the confusion of many voices arguing.

Obstacle 7: Previous failure (Mark 9:17–18)

A definition of insanity is trying again to do the same thing in the same way but expecting different results. There has been some criticism of churches that keep trying the same old methods to reach out that have not worked before, but somehow expect that it will be different this time. On the other hand there are those in churches who come out with that adage, 'we've tried that before and it didn't work'. For example, a church might run an Alpha course but fail to produce any fruit from it all. It would be unwise to simply do the course the same way again and hope that things might work out better. On the other hand it would also be unwise to conclude that Alpha courses do not produce any good results. Clearly in many places they have been the means of bringing quite a number of people to Christ. It would also be unwise to draw the conclusion that Alpha courses will not work in that church's setting. The best course of action would be to look at why the course did not produce any good results, and ask what could be done differently? It may be that the same church could run another course, but with different leaders, proper prayer support and using a different location, and find that it is very fruitful.

No-one likes to fail – though a bit of failure throughout our lives is usually necessary to break down the pride of our hearts, forming in us the humility that God looks for. How we react to failures is of crucial importance. We might simply give up, blaming ourselves and feeling altogether miserable. We could give up, but make excuses shifting the blame somewhere else. Or we could try again, learning from the past and making any necessary adjustments.

The father of the boy in this passage could have reacted to the disciples' inability to cast out the demon in a variety of ways. He could have given up, thinking it had been worth a shot, but just did not work. You may be praying for someone or some situation and nothing is happening. What do you do? Do you give up? Do you persevere? Do you conclude that it could not have been God's will? Now that might be the case depending on what it was you asked for, but it is God's will to save people (2 Peter 3:9), and to set them free (Luke 4:18). It is God's will that we see revival and spiritual awakening in our land. It is not that he is unwilling to answer, but that we are slow to cry out, or lack the true desire that he looks for. God does have his timing for things, but that being the case it is vital that we do not give up.

Obstacle 8: A measure of unbelief (Mark 9:22–24)
The father brought his son to the disciples of Jesus in the first place because he must have heard of the reports about their ministry, giving him a measure of faith and hope. Jesus had already sent his disciples out on occasions, and they had driven out many demons (Mark 6:13). So why could the disciples not cast the demon out on this occasion?

This passage raises a number of interesting points and we shall look at some of these as we go on. Some have assumed that Jesus was suggesting that to cast out this particular 'kind' of demon required prayer and fasting beforehand. Prayer and fasting will prove to be a great aid in much of our ministry whether in preaching, healing, or casting out demons. However, it may be a wrong assumption to presume this is what Jesus meant. We must be careful not to build too strong a case on this passage, and certainly not get legalistic about having to pray and fast before any deliverance session. Some cases where there is a need to drive out a demon can come by surprise!

Apart from the fact that not all the early manuscripts of this passage contain the word 'fasting', there is also some question as to what Jesus was referring to when he said, 'this kind'. Although there is a definite hierarchy in the demonic ranks, I think it is questionable to suggest that some demons require prayer and fasting and others do not. Though, as I have said, the practice of prayer and fasting is a real benefit in such ministry, I also believe that Jesus has given us authority over all the power of the evil one (see Luke 9:1; Matthew 28:18), and the name of Jesus will triumph over any demon. The greatest problem in driving out demons is not the strength of the demon, but the condition of the person concerned, and whether they have any unconfessed sin, or are holding unforgiveness towards someone, or have some other 'block' in their life, or maybe the condition of the person praying!

So what else could Jesus have meant by his words, 'this kind'?

The problem that Jesus clearly identifies in this whole passage is one of unbelief. It could be that prayer (and fasting) are actually required to overcome unbelief. When that is overcome then in faith we can minister in the power of the Spirit and the authority of Jesus name. Whatever is concluded about the meaning of Jesus words in verse 29, the truth is that unbelief was the real issue in this episode (Mark 9:19).

The father's unbelief

The father had some belief or he would not have been there with his son in the first place. However, his faith has been dealt a blow leaving him in some doubt when Jesus appears on the scene. This doubt is expressed in his statement to Jesus in verse 22, and Jesus picks him up on this, declaring that *'everything is possible for him who believes.'* The father responds with the famous saying, *'I do believe; help me overcome my unbelief.'* This response has become so well known in the Church as it is a sentiment with which all of us have been able to identify at some point.

We can believe in God, and believe in his ability to act and save, deliver and heal, in a general way. We believe what we read that he has done in the Scriptures. We believe that God has moved in mighty ways throughout history, and that he may be doing great works in parts of the earth today. The question is: do you believe God will act today, in your situation, in your community, in response to your prayers?

The disciples' unbelief

As we noted earlier, Jesus took Peter, James and John with him up the mountain. He took only the three of them into Jairus' house with him, and on other occasions too he only took this inner group with him. It was not a matter of favouritism, but of training, and spending most time with those who would take leading roles later on. That left the other nine down below. Though they had seen many of Jesus miracles, they may not have had the same faith level as the other three disciples. Clearly their faith was lacking on this occasion.

If we are to see God move in power in our land in response to prevailing prayer, then it is important that we do not just have some believing individuals, but also believing churches. I see in the nine disciples a parallel to the church today where there is in some places a lack of experience of God at work, and a lack of expectancy that God will work.

The rise of so much counterfeit, occult activity in our day is partly due to the huge gap the Church has often left by not operating in the anointing and power of the Holy Spirit. It is a great shame that people go to false spiritual healers because they do not know of a church that prays for the sick.

The unbelieving generation

There is still one further obstacle, namely living in an unbelieving culture and atmosphere. Even where we find believing individual Christians, and faith-filled, expectant churches, we are still ministering in a nation and prevailing culture that is largely ungodly and unbelieving. The power of the media and other influences create scepticism in relation to the power of a Personal God. While God can move in power in any situation, as Jesus showed in this instance, our ministry is usually aided by an atmosphere of faith. Much prayer and praise enhance such an atmosphere. In a society where pleasure, the love of money, and sexual gratification are widely praised as the goals and gods of life, there needs to be a great increase of prayer and praise of the living God to combat these idols, and change the spiritual climate.

The father's responses

1. Pressed in to Jesus

The first obstacle – that of the previous failure – was overcome largely because Jesus turned up just in time. The father of the boy did not give up, but pressed in to seek Jesus' help, though somewhat tentatively.

We must not let past experiences define reality for us and limit our belief in what is possible. Jesus never fails, and all things are possible through faith in him. We must allow God's Word to shape our belief system and define the boundaries of what can happen. Too easily we can be shaped by our own experiences.

I used to sell chocolate for a large UK company. One day I called on a small supermarket in a very depressed looking little town. One glance at the half-empty shelves suggested that this shop was not doing well. I was greeted by the elderly store manager with the words, 'sweeties don't sell anymore, son.' Was his statement true or not? From his perspective, and in his situation, there was little demand for the products I was selling. The truth was that 'sweeties' did sell very well, and still do, much to the frustration of many a dentist, and doing much damage to many a diet!

Similarly we can get pulled down by previous negative experiences and failures into an unbelieving, but quite false perspective. We need to pay heed to the words of God on the mountain and listen to his Son. What does he say to us?

> *'Everything is possible for him who believes.'*   (Mark 9:23)

> *'I tell you the truth, anyone who has faith in me will do what I have been doing. He will do even greater things than these, because I am going to the Father.'*   (John 14:12)

'You may ask me for anything in my name, and I will do it.'
                                            (John 14:14)

'Therefore I tell you, whatever you ask for in prayer, believe that you have received it, and it will be yours.' (Mark 10:24)

Who are you going to believe?

2. Sought more faith

The father knew he had a problem with unbelief and asked Jesus to help him. It's as simple as that – ask for it. Ask the Lord to help.

Of course you may discover that you already have faith and that the real need is for you to exercise it. The disciples asked Jesus to increase their faith (Luke 17:5), to which Jesus responds, *'If you have faith as small as a mustard seed, you can say to this mulberry tree, "Be uprooted and planted in the sea," and it will obey you'* (Luke 17:6). We do not need to already have great faith to begin to pray and ask God for big answers. Even a little faith will bring about mighty acts, and the more we pray in faith and see answers, so the more our faith will grow. Just as our muscles will grow and develop with good exercise, so too will our faith.

Remember, our faith is not some 'force' but faith in Someone, in our God. Therefore it is helpful to focus our eyes on the Lord, being impressed with everything about him, and giving ourselves to praise him. Praise and worship cause our faith to grow as it draws our minds away from our perspective of life, and focuses on God, drawing us into viewing life and all its challenges in relation to the might and majesty of the Almighty.

There is no obstacle to Jesus, and he drives out the demon and sets the boy free. We notice a number of interesting points in the way Jesus deals with this situation.

• **Jesus does not give undue attention to the demonic**. Verse 25 says, *'a crowd was running to the scene,'* and Jesus responded by immediately dispatching the demon.

- **Jesus identifies the spirit**. The father had stated that the spirit *'robbed the boy of speech'*, but Jesus calls it a deaf and mute spirit. He knew this by revelation of the Holy Spirit.
- **The act of deliverance was violent**. Even with Jesus' authority operating, the act of deliverance was still noisy and violent, leaving some thinking that the boy was dead.

We would do well to learn from this. Though the content of the passages we have looked at in this section have caused us to talk a fair amount about the battle against demonic forces, we should not give undue attention to them. We must recognise the battle, and at times expose the work of the enemy, but our focus in the battle must always be on our Commander, the Lord Jesus Christ.

We need to listen to the revelation that the Holy Spirit brings to us so that we can pray in line with God's will, and go beyond what we see with our own eyes and know by our own understanding.

Finally, as we pray for the transformation of our communities, and a spiritual awakening throughout our nations, there will be a degree of violent encounter in the clash of the kingdoms. It may be messy at times, but the outcome is sure, and the final victory is the Lord's.

We have an open invitation and right of access into the throne room of God. There are obstacles that get put in the way at times, but obstacles are there to be overcome.

> *'Build up, build up, prepare the road!*
> *Remove the obstacles out of the way of my people.'*
> (Isaiah 57:14)

Those we have looked at in these three chapters were very ordinary people who displayed varying degrees of faith. They were however determined parents who longed to see their children set free and healed. God is looking for ordinary people today, who have a similar determination, to pray in extraordinary ways that will usher in his Kingdom rule.

SECTION 3

Prioritising Prayer

Introduction

Much of what has been written in this book so far has been concerning persevering in intercessory prayer for individuals and whole communities. There are, of course, other types of prayer, and it is important to develop a balanced prayer life. This will include intercession, plus devotional prayer and worship, biblical meditation, personal petitions, listening to God and more. There are other good books that cover many of these aspects of prayer.

In this final section I want to issue the challenge to prioritise prayer in our lives and in our churches, and encourage the inclusion of prayer as an integral part of evangelism. In no way do I wish to make anyone feel guilty about his or her lack of prayer. I believe that grace motivates us in a much healthier way than being pressurised by guilt.

Already we have seen that there are many struggles in prayer, and all of us have found difficulty at times, maybe all the time. I am certainly one who struggles, but I am believing that God will give me the grace as I seek to obey his call upon my life, and the Scriptural exhortations to *'devote ourselves to prayer'* (see Colossians 4:2).

Chapter 7

Rescheduling Around Prayer

I have been in many meetings where there had been an intention to spend some significant time in prayer, but we have all talked too much and the prayer has been squeezed in at the end. It can be the same in our lives where we have good intentions about spending time in prayer, but something else comes up and the prayer slot goes. I have found this to be a continual battle in my life and ministry. I do believe and practise praying while on the move, and Scripture speaks of 'praying continually', which suggests maintaining a constant attitude of prayer. However, if we are to pray in such a way that 'moves mountains and mulberry trees' then we need to give significant and focused time to prayer. Token prayers at the end of meetings will not do.

In this struggle I sensed the Lord speak to me. First, in a dream I was given the impression that I needed to spend half my 'working time' in prayer. Now this would be quite impractical for most people, but God had called me to lead a Prayer Ministry and it does not seem unreasonable then that a great amount of my time be spent in prayer. Let me say that I struggled miserably to do this. In case anyone thinks prayer is an easy option, I can assure you that I have found working much easier and less strenuous than praying!

Second, I sensed the Lord say to me to 'reschedule my life around prayer.' What he seemed to be saying was that I should stop trying to fit prayer in, but start with prayer then schedule everything else around it. Whether we are praying for several hours each week or just a few minutes a day, we can all schedule in the prayer first at a sensible time and make every effort to keep to it. Many people have found that the Prayer Wall has helped them to do this, and we shall talk more about this later.

Even when we do set time for prayer, and manage to keep that time, there are other difficulties with which we have to deal. I am an active person, I like being busy, I enjoy my work. When I pray my mind often wanders, ideas of something I could preach on suddenly come to me, thoughts of things I need to do flood into my mind. Then there is the problem of the phone ringing – I could ignore it, or maybe should have unplugged it. The doorbell rings, or something else distracts me. At times it seems there is a plan afoot to stop me praying!

The problems of discipline, disruptions, distractions and drowsiness

We conducted a survey of people of various ages from a variety of churches in our area. We asked what people felt were the things that hindered them the most from spending time in prayer. We gave them a list of twelve possible hindrances, asking them to rate each one as to whether it hindered them a lot, sometimes, rarely, or never. Four of the choices stood out clearly as the hindrances people encountered the most and the following percentages are those who indicated that that particular area hindered them at times or a lot:

* 76% stated lack of discipline
* 71% indicated disruptions and distractions
* 58% said tiredness, or growing faint easily
* 52% indicated a lack of time

We shall outline the problems that seem to occur and affect

many of us here, then at the end of the chapter shall suggest some ways of overcoming these difficulties.

The discipline issue

Clearly some people are more disciplined and organised than others, but when it comes to prayer most of us can have a problem here. Prayer is a spiritual battle and our foe will use the discipline problem all he can. I also believe that even the most disorganised of us can find the grace from God to discipline ourselves in prayer.

2 Timothy 1:7 says,

> *'For God did not give us a spirit of timidity, but a spirit of power, of love and of self-discipline.'*

Discipline can be seen as something stern, difficult and lacking in any joy. Richard Foster's acclaimed book *Celebration of Discipline* helped many of us to see the spiritual disciplines – such as prayer, fasting, meditation – in a new light. Good discipline is a healthy asset to our lives, and it need not become a legalistic burden. Discipline is a great aid in persevering prayer.

Having a perceived lack of time for prayer is closely related to the issue of discipline. We all have the same number of hours in the week, though some people have many more demands on their lives than others. Sometimes busy folk are better at fitting in extra activities because their schedules force them to be organised and disciplined. Often it is a case of motivation. People invariably find time for what they really want to do.

However, we must not be too harsh on ourselves. If a mother of three pre-school age children finds it hard to find an hour a day for prayer that is not surprising. We do need to prioritise prayer in such a way that we redeem some of the less productive times in our week. Dare I suggest that some Christians watch too much television?

Disruptions and distractions

Depending on our home and family circumstances, and depending on where we go to pray, the amount of potential disruptions and distractions may vary considerably. Some people have developed a greater ability to focus in prayer that they seem unaware of disruptions or noise around them. Others are easily distracted, and some have minds that seem to wander everywhere except where they are supposed to be.

I do not think I am alone in finding that when I set myself to pray, I could almost guarantee the phone or doorbell ringing.

Drowsiness

I think it is quite a common experience that when we begin to pray we can suddenly feel quite drowsy and just want to go to sleep. This will happen more if we pray late in the day or when we are physically tired, but the feeling of growing faint can come over us in an unexpected way when we get into a serious prayer time. This is because prayer is a spiritual battle.

Before seeking to give some helps in overcoming these difficulties it would be good to take a look at the patterns of Jesus' prayer life and that of the apostles.

Jesus' prayer patterns

I am impressed by the prayer life of Jesus and the example of the way he prioritised his relationship with the Father. The hallmark of his life was his intimacy with the Father, and the first priority he gave to his disciples was to be with him. We read in Mark 3:14–15,

> *'He appointed twelve – designating them apostles – that **they** **might be with him** and that he might send them out to preach and to have authority to drive out demons.'*
>
> (emphasis added)

On reading these verses we can easily miss the words I have highlighted. We are so used to looking to see where the action is that we quickly focus on the activities of preaching and casting out demons. The first activity for the disciples was spending time with Jesus and growing in their relationship with him. In whatever ministry a person is called to it is vitally important that they make 'being with Jesus' their highest priority. This is true for preachers, evangelists, pastors, and also for intercessors. It is possible to engage in lots of intercessory prayer, praying for many people and needs, but not have a close relationship with the Lord himself. As Mike Bickle of Kansas City has often said, 'Intimacy precedes intercession.' Prayers of intercession will become increasingly effective when we first draw near to the Lord in an intimate way. We will be sustained in intercession by our relationship with him. It is important that we do not plunge into lots of intercessory prayer because of the great volume of need all around, but first take time to simply be with Jesus. Out of that growing relationship of intimacy we shall hear his voice more clearly, and pray what is on his heart for us to pray. We must not fall into the trap of running to the agenda of need, but must listen for the Lord's agenda.

Jesus met the needs of many people but he also kept the priorities of his ministry, seeking the Father's face and running to his agenda (see Luke 4:42–44).

Jesus regularly got alone to pray (Mark 1:35; Luke 5:16)
This was clearly a frequent and disciplined practice in his life. Jesus made the effort and sacrifice to get alone with his Father. It is good to pray with others but it is vital to get alone with God at times. Jesus had many demands on his time with crowds often pursuing him, but he got up very early or found some remote place in order to keep his valued priority of communing with the Father.

Jesus sustained prayer at crucial times (Luke 6:12–16; 22:39–46)
Before choosing his twelve disciples, which was a major decision for him, Jesus spent the night in prayer. We might

avoid some regrets if we spent more time praying over important decisions.

When facing the forthcoming agony of the cross Jesus went out and spent considerable time and energy in prayer. The disciples fell asleep while Jesus sweated drops of blood. Crucial times require sustained prayer.

Jesus prayed privately with his disciples (Luke 9:18, 28–29; 11:1–2)

Jesus got alone to pray and he also prayed with his disciples present. The prayer life of their Master clearly impressed the disciples as they asked him to teach them to pray.

Jesus prayed with real passion (Luke 19:41–44)

Jesus wept over the city of Jerusalem. He felt passionately for the people. We need his heart for our towns and cities that we might *'sow in tears and reap with songs of joy'* (Psalm 126:5).

Jesus prayed for his disciples (Luke 22:31–32)

Satan asked to sift the disciples and though God allowed this for a purpose, Jesus prayed for them, and especially for Simon Peter, who, though he would go through a real test, would come back to strengthen the others. It is most important for leaders to pray for those around them in their church leadership or team.

The apostles prayer patterns in Acts

The apostles had been around Jesus long enough that the importance of the vital link with God through prayer must have been firmly established in their minds. We see this is the case looking at the patterns of prayer they followed in the book of Acts.

Extraordinary prayer (1:14)

After Jesus ascended the disciples had to wait for the promised Holy Spirit to come. The one thing they could do was pray. They gave themselves to constant and united prayer. In any circumstance we can always pray. We must not wait passively for God's promises to be fulfilled but be active in praying for their fulfilment. The early Church prepared for and helped usher in Pentecost with prayer.

Prioritised prayer (2:42; 6:4)
Prayer was one of the key foundations of the life of the early Church, alongside the apostles' teaching, fellowship and the breaking of bread. The apostles were most concerned when other duties might take up their time in such a way that they would neglect prayer and the ministry of the Word of God. This is a constant need for leaders of churches today. So many other needs and tasks can take up, not only our time, but also our focus. We must keep the priorities in place with church members recognising their part and helping their leaders to do this.

Regular prayer times (3:1; 10:9)
Peter and John went up to the Temple at one of the set hours of prayer. They clearly practised a regular and disciplined pattern of prayer. Within such a practice came the opportunity for a miraculous healing that would lead to many coming to faith. Peter also prays at the noon hour and within this discipline God speaks to him through a vision that will dramatically alter the course of the Church.

When we practise regular prayer then we give room for God to break into our lives in miraculous ways.

Crisis prayer (4:23–30; 12:5; 16:25)
Some people only pray when they are in trouble or some crisis occurs. Sometimes in a critical situation fear and anxiety can take over and we fail to pray. The apostles and the early Church had prioritised prayer so it was the natural response in any crisis. When threatened, persecuted or imprisoned they turned to God in prayer, often with amazing results.

Prayer using the laying on of hands (6:6; 8:17; 13:3; 19:6)
The apostles also prayed with people accompanied by the

laying on of their hands. This was one means by which the Holy Spirit was imparted and a means for healing the sick.

Accompanied prayer with fasting and worship (13:1–3)
Finally, we see that the apostles practised fasting and worshipping the Lord along with their praying. Worship brings us into an awareness of God's presence that greatly encourages our praying, and fasting adds a definite power to prayer.

So we see from the lives of Jesus and his apostles that prayer was a clear priority for them. They had regular, disciplined times of prayer, plus some extraordinary occasions when they prayed at great length. Jesus, with all the demands on his time, especially made sure he got alone in prayer where he was less likely to be disturbed or distracted, and he challenged his sleepy disciples to be alert, watching and praying.

We might find good examples in the lives of Jesus and the apostles, and desire to follow their patterns but find it a hard thing to do. First, we must have a genuine belief in the value of prayer and a true desire to pray. This desire may not be strong but it can grow. That is the starting point. From there the Holy Spirit will give us grace as we humble ourselves, recognising our need of his help. God gives grace to the humble. In this grace we can overcome the problems that hinder our prayer life.

Overcoming the discipline problem

We might pray when something seriously goes wrong in our lives or when we have been greatly motivated by an anointed sermon. In the more ordinary times of our lives we will not engage in significant times of prayer unless we plan to do so or have made it a regular practice of our days.

There can be a downside to regular, disciplined times of prayer. Like in other regular activities in life we can get to a point where we simply go through the motions. It is important to 'add firewood to our prayer life every day' (see Leviticus 6:12–13) through the Scriptures and other aids. It is also crucial not to get too hung up about our discipline such that we lose the true spirit of prayer. Jesus and the apostles were disciplined in prayer, but also prayed in a variety of ways and at different times. The real key was that they made prayer a priority.

Training yourself

Paul urges Timothy, *'train yourself to be godly'* (1 Timothy 4:7). It is possible and necessary for us to train ourselves in godly ways, including prayer. I believe strongly in the power of prayer, and can be highly motivated at times to pray. There are other times, however, when I am not so inspired and this is when the value of training comes in. Over the years I have sought to train myself by studying the Scriptures, reading many books on prayer, listening to those who have developed strong prayer lives and ministries, and practising different forms of prayer.

'Appointments with God'

If you make an appointment with your dentist it is most likely that you will turn up at the surgery at that time. If you think to yourself that you really do need to go to the dentist for a check up sometime you may not get round to it. When we make important appointments with people we tend to keep them. To help discipline ourselves in prayer we can 'make an appointment' with God. If we take this seriously, recognising he is more important than any person, then there is a strong likelihood we will keep that time. We must not let other things interfere with that time, barring any real emergencies. This is one of the strengths of the Prayer Wall. The individual watchman's hour slot is like a weekly appointment with God. It is not their only prayer time but often one that they otherwise would not have made. My parents are both on the 'Wall'. They take their hours very seriously making sure that they do not arrange anything else for that time. For them this works very well. While encouraging people to take an hour on the 'Wall' we do suggest they do not get too legalistic about it, and should feel free to take an occasional holiday. The general discipline of this practice is usually of great benefit to the intercessor.

A person may not feel able to sign up for the same hour every week but I would still encourage making at least one such appointment every week, even if at various times or on different days.

Accountability

This term can be unpopular with some, and raises fears in others who may have experienced 'heavy shepherding' in the past. However, we are all accountable, first to God, and also to each other in the Body of Christ. Seen in the right, biblical light, accountability is both healthy and helpful. I am only too pleased to have a core team of leaders to whom Helen and I are accountable. There is nothing oppressive about this, in fact quite the opposite is true as I feel I have the freedom to try things, knowing that they are there to help correct and guide when necessary.

Some may react and say that prayer is a personal matter between the person concerned and God. I believe by taking that line such a person loses out on valuable help and strengthening. It is not a matter of someone else telling you what to do, or prying into your life in unwelcome ways. It is simply a case of giving someone else who you trust the permission to speak into your life and ask you how your prayer life is doing. They are not heaping condemnation on you. They are helping you examine yourself. Husbands and wives can help each other in this, or trusted friends, pastors, home group leaders or anyone else you trust and know has your interests at heart, wanting to see you grow in the Lord.

Using a journal

A way of being accountable to yourself is by keeping a prayer journal. It is also a great means of disciplining yourself and keeping a record of what you have prayed for, what has been answered and what God has been saying to you. I get an extra diary at the start of the year – one with enough room for each day to write a good few sentences. I record the daily Bible passages that I read, making any notes from them. I write down any other notable happenings during the day, any sense of what God is saying, any significant dreams I have, and any answers to prayer. I find that this journal gives me a great source of inspiration, and I often look back over it reminding myself of important revelations and activities.

Overcoming disruptions and distractions

There is no shortage of disturbances that will interfere with our praying. It is wise therefore to find a good place and a good time to pray. For some a room in your house is fine, for others it is beneficial to get outdoors (I have prayed through many a park or wood accompanied by my dog). There are church buildings open at times for quiet prayer. It is important to find a place that is suitable and reasonably free from distractions.

Again, what is the best time will vary from person to person. Early morning is good for many, having the advantages of being before anyway else is up in the house and before the phone or doorbell is likely to ring. It's a great way to start the day, even just one day per week.

When my children were younger I used to find a late evening time of prayer was very helpful once everyone else was well settled in bed. In more recent times my older teenagers have the capacity to stay up much later than me, so being up first is now a better option.

Things we need to get done that day can distract our minds. Sometimes it is best to get such things out of the way first. Our thoughts can go all over the place and we feel we are failing to focus properly in prayer. Do not put yourself down for that as most of us find this happens. It is important to not get put off but keep getting our mind back to the matters of prayer. Even only a few minutes of really focused prayer can bring mighty results.

Overcoming drowsiness (the fainting spirit)

In the garden of Gethsemane Jesus found his disciples, *'sleeping, because their eyes were heavy'* (Mark 14:40). This heaviness and sleepiness can be a peculiarly common experience when we set ourselves to pray. How can we overcome this?

A garment of praise

Isaiah 61:3 contains these words of what God will give us: *'a garment of praise instead of a spirit of despair'*. Other translations speak of *'a spirit of heaviness'* and the Hebrew term could be translated *'a fainting spirit'*. When we go to battle in prayer we can easily succumb to a fainting spirit. God has provided the antidote and it is *'a garment of praise'*. It is praise that releases joy and strength, and drives the enemy away. We need to clothe ourselves in this garment in order to know the victory over this heaviness.

Practically we need to focus on the wonderful attributes of the Lord, and sing praise to him. This may be fine for musicians and singers but what about the ones who are not exactly tuneful? Well I am one of the least tuneful folk around but I can still sing to the Lord and my voice is sweet to him (see Song of Songs 2:14). I often use tapes or discs of worship songs to help me.

A good position

If you lie in bed and pray you are more likely to doze off than someone walking through a park. If you are tired and close your eyes to pray then that can be it. I would suggest that in the fight against sleepiness in prayer that it is helpful to pray with your eyes open and also to stand and walk around. It is good to close your eyes and kneel in prayer at times as well, but not so good when you are struggling with tiredness.

Discipline becoming delight

While the above points will be helpful in developing our prayer life, the real key for us is delighting in the Lord and in being in his Presence. Prayer must not, and need not be religious drudgery. Prayer is an adventure. It is touching the throne of heaven. It is getting hold of the Father's heart.

It is a relationship, communicating with our loving Heavenly Father. It is a deep spiritual experience rather than the repetition of certain words (though we may repeat some prayers at times it is vital our heart is in such words).

Developing discipline is good, and overcoming some of the other hindrances to prayer may be most helpful, but we could do this and still have no real heart for prayer. God is not looking for well-disciplined lives but for hearts that truly love him and are growing in appreciation of his grace. If we are to see great breakthroughs come through prayer we will need to give serious time to this pursuit but we must always remember that the heart issue is paramount.

> *'Delight yourselves in the LORD,*
> *and he will give you the desires of your heart.'*
>
> (Psalm 37:4)

Our calling is first to be with him. When we delight ourselves in him we will want to be with him. This relationship of delight is key for us as I have already said in previous chapters. As we grow in our understanding of the Lord's delight in us, so we are freed from our insecurities, and can delight in him more fully. When two people fall in love they delight in each other's company, longing to be together. So as we delight in our Saviour, and know his delight in us as his bride it will have the following effects:

- We will desire to spend more time with him in worship, prayer and simply being in his Presence. When I first met Helen I did not have to discipline myself to make time to see her. I wanted to enough that not much was likely to get in the way.
- We will be increasingly devoted to our Lord. Our minds and hearts will be focused more completely on him; therefore we will not be so easily distracted or disturbed. His beauty will have captured our hearts and our attention.
- We will have a new alertness and joy in his Presence that will defeat the weariness and fainting spirit.

God has been giving to the Church a new degree of grace to sustain extraordinary prayer. This has enabled some to maintain early morning prayer or spend all night praying. God gives the grace; we need to respond by rescheduling our lives in such a way that prayer is given a place of true priority.

Chapter 8

Invest in Prayer

If we are to build bridges of prayer and form canopies of prayer then we need to invest in prayer. If we believe that prayer is a necessary foundation for our entire ministry then we need to seriously invest time, energy, space and finances into prayer. While many churches say that 'prayer is the powerhouse', and come out with other fine sounding phrases, the truth is that their investment of resources often betrays such statements. C. Peter Wagner says, 'I would guess that 90 per cent of the churches in America have no line item for prayer in their budget.' He then quotes Jesus words, *'where your treasure is, there your heart will be also'* (Matthew 6:21), and draws the conclusion that, 'churches with no budget for prayer may well have little heart for prayer.'[1] Churches will often invest in pastoral ministry, youth work, administration and mission – all worthy of investment – but invest so little in prayer. Churches will pay an administrator, but few have considered releasing a full-time intercessor. Why is this?

Investing financially in prayer

It might be argued that intercessory prayer is a ministry for the whole body, not just a specialised few. I totally agree. Evangelism and even pastoring are also works for the whole body to engage in, yet we consider having full-time pastors and evangelists. Part of their function is to equip the rest of the

Church; likewise a full-time intercessor or prayer leader will seek to equip the whole body to pray more effectively. Of course they would not need to be in full-time supported ministry to do this, but I believe there is a case for this on occasions just as much as their is a case for full-time supported administrators or youth workers. There are some difficulties in the way we have often thought about this in the church that need to be addressed.

The problem of needing measurable results

Wise investors will want some evidence that the money they are putting into a company or project is going to bring about a good return. There are two crucial differences between the Church and the business world. First, in the Church we give, not necessarily expecting any return, although God often blesses a generous giver, but a truly generous giver gives because it is right to give not in order to get something back.

Second, we give to, that is financially support and therefore invest in, what we believe God has told us to, and believe is right in his sight. Prayer, especially for citywide transformation, may take considerable time to produce its fruit. In fact when we begin to seriously focus prayer on a situation it may well get worse before it gets better.

The problem of seeing prayer as spiritual and not needing financial resource

It seems that money can be put into almost any type of Christian ministry, except prayer. Somehow prayer can be viewed as an 'other worldly' exercise, therefore not being a ministry requiring any financial investment. Wagner's words at the start of this chapter suggest that if churches have no budget for prayer then they may have little heart for prayer. That could be so but it may be that many churches have simply never thought to invest money into prayer ministry. The reason for this chapter is to put forward a case for starting to think about this in a new way.

People who pray a lot are sometimes considered to be too heavenly minded to be of any earthly use. A person can become a bit too detached from everyday life and seem to have their head in the clouds, but I believe that true prayer is firmly rooted in earthly life and aware of the needs of people. I think the truth is that we need to become so heavenly minded that we are of incredible earthly use, as we bring the needs of earth to heaven and the mind of heaven to earth.

The problem that much of our investment can be selfish

Many Christians give unselfishly and sacrificially. However, there is still an element of 'selfish giving' in our churches. There is the problem that some believers do not give in anything like a generous manner. But the problem I want to address here is the willingness of people and churches to invest in what they see will benefit them and their church, while there can be an unwillingness to give to ministry that we do not perceive will help us in any way. (Some mission agencies may also have felt this to be so.)

While each church needs to seek God and use their money wisely under the direction of the Holy Spirit, I think it is pertinent to raise some questions:

- How many growing churches employ another pastor or church worker rather than support a church planter or a missionary?
- How much of our giving goes to maintaining our church ministry compared to giving to the poor?
- Do some believers give to their church believing that they then have a right to expect the pastor to be there for them if they need him?
- Do churches get a better response for an appeal for their new building or sound system than they would for an appeal to help another church or a foreign crisis? If so, why?

There is a side to the joy of giving that cannot be experienced until we give away generously expecting nothing in return. When we do this God usually blesses us anyway but that should not be the motive for the gift.

Many years ago Helen and I visited Kenya, ministering in several churches. After returning home we started to receive letters from a Kenyan pastor. I could not think who he was and had been warned to be careful about any requests for money. He persisted in writing for some time though he never actually asked for financial support. I prayed about this and felt God say to send him a gift. We took up a small offering at the church and sent it to him. Almost immediately after doing this our church received an unexpected gift from another source. This sort of thing happened several times.

We need to give to what or who God tells us to regardless of the perceived benefit or lack of benefit. I say 'perceived' because regarding prayer and investing in such ministry, we will all receive a benefit.

God's provision for us
I believe God called Helen and me to invest our lives at this time in the prayer ministry. The implications of this for us financially were that we would have to leave the church manse (their property) and stop receiving a regular stipend from the church. We had to find another house for a family of five people, and find financial support. We have never asked for money and I can honestly say we have never gone without. We have some marvellous supporters who give to us regularly and we also receive some unexpected gifts, often just when they are needed. We have been able to rent houses when necessary and now share a good house with my parents.

I believe God called us to be pioneers and to break open a new concept of ministry. While we were not to ask for money, I believe that is so that we can speak out for other intercessors who may be called to full-time intercessory ministry without anyone thinking we are looking to gain out of this for ourselves.

Some might argue from our very testimony that if God calls someone to a full-time ministry of prayer then God will supply. Maybe he will, but do we apply that same logic to pastors or other paid ministry positions?

How do we invest our money in prayer ministry?

Part of our vision is to see people released to spend significant quantities of time in prayer for our city. Some already do this, and a person does not have to be financially supported to do so, e.g. retired people or people who give large portions of their leisure time to prayer. If we are to see the covering of prayer extended and the volume of prayer increased, then we do need to release more people for more time in prayer.

This is not a cop out for those who might be involved. Prayer is hard work. I would expect intercessors to work as hard as any other person. Epaphras worked hard for the Colossian church as he *'wrestled in prayer'* for them (see Colossians 4:12–13). No one should think such a calling to prayer ministry would be easy. It will be a tremendous battle. There will be hard tests and the need of much discipline.

Churches need to consider the possibilities of expanding prayer ministry in a variety of ways. One is releasing someone as an intercessor. There are others too, for example, investing in good prayer materials, equipping seminars or prayer rooms.

Dutch Sheets, who has written some of the best books on prayer, says this: 'Churches must be willing to pay the price for a first-class, organised, informed, visible, attractive prayer ministry.'[2]

However, we must not make the mistake of thinking that simply putting money into prayer ministry will give our church a dynamic prayer life. There must first be a real vision and heart for prayer.

Investing space for prayer

Churches that have their own premises tend to give away a lot about their values and priorities by the design and layout of their building. As you enter a church building you might see a large pulpit or a platform with many musical instruments.

Prayer rooms

I am aware of a growing number of churches setting aside a room on their premises as a prayer room. This is a most encouraging trend highlighting a growing sense of the importance of prayer. At the time of writing we are developing a prayer room in the city centre of Glasgow.

Church buildings open

There is also a slow but increasing number of church buildings open for prayer during the days of the week. While it can be good that church premises are well used for community activities, it would be a shame if we altogether lost the value of our buildings as places for quiet reflection and prayer. Helen and I discovered that our local Presbyterian church has its sanctuary and a small chapel open through the week, and we have found this a valuable place to go to and pray.

Investing time in prayer

We can be fooled into thinking that we do not have time to pray more, supposing that we would get less done if we stopped to pray. I tend to find that giving time to prayer results in my being much more productive in everything else I do.

Redeeming the time

There can be much wasted time in our lives. We need time to work, to relate to people (especially close family), time to eat, time to relax and time to sleep. There is a time for everything. There may be times in our lives that we do not use for any of these necessary and productive pursuits. Getting up an hour early once a week or missing one dinner a week and spending the time in prayer, are quite possible for most of us.

Re-examining your church and ministry involvement

Being very busy in Christian ministry can appear commendable. The question we have to ask ourselves every so often is this: is all our activity bearing any fruit? There are times that it is right to persevere faithfully when no result is coming forth. But there are also times when we must honestly conclude that what we are expending ourselves on may not be what God wants us to do.

Giving time to prayer in church gatherings

Prayer is one of the key foundations of the Church (Acts 2:42). How much time does it get in church gatherings? I have been to 'prayer meetings' where there was a half-hour sermon, much talk, but only a very few minutes of prayer. We need a good biblical balance of praise, preaching, prayer and other ministries in our gatherings. Again Wagner says, 'With a few notable exceptions, prayer in local churches has amounted to little more than tokenism.'[3] Some may feel his comment is too critical and harsh but my experience would suggest that he does have a point. In some church meetings there seems to be the sense that prayer needs to be made in order to give the appearance that things are being done in the right way. The question is whether or not such prayer is really heartfelt. If we only make token gestures of prayer then we would be better not bothering. Such prayers give a false sense of spiritual life to the people but make no impression elsewhere. What we need in our churches is what Wesley Duewel passionately states in his book *Mighty Prevailing Prayer*: 'We need a new intense and radical commitment to prayer, leaders who know and prove the power of prayer, congregations growing ever more mighty in prayer. We need prevailing leadership to mould a new generation of prayer warriors.'[4]

Pastors[5] investing in prayer

As we saw in the last chapter both Jesus and his apostles gave themselves to prayer as a clear and valued priority in their lives. In Acts 6:4 the apostles make it very plain that they should not get caught up by the demands of people's needs but first give their time to prayer and the ministry of the Word. This needs to continue to be the priority and the practice today.

On the one hand I know that it is not easy for pastors to keep to the priorities that they intended to when sudden and sometimes very great needs arise in the lives of the congregation. However, there needs to be discernment about what the pastor should attend to and what can be attended to by others, such as elders or house group leaders. The temptations to meet certain demands so as to keep folks happy, or even for the pastor to justify himself, must be avoided.

On the other hand, although many pastors are busy people, there is a certain degree of choice about what they invest in during their ministry. Some may read much or engage in some study, others will invest time in conferences. I would encourage pastors to seriously invest time in developing a dynamic personal prayer life. I have always sought to have at least one day a week to spend in personal devotion, intercession and seeking the Lord.

First and foremost the churches need their key leaders to be men and women who walk close to the Lord, spending significant time in prayer and discerning God's word and vision for their flocks. Second I believe the pastors of any area need to gather together regularly to pray for their community and to support one another in prayer.

Releasing pastors to pray

If church members want leaders who are people of prayer, hearing from God and bringing fresh words, revelation and direction to the Body, then those members need to be serious about helping release their pastors for this priority of prayer. There needs to be support from the Body, and an active encouragement, almost insistence from the wider leadership, for the pastor to have a significant portion of time for prayer and meditation on the Word. This means relieving the pressures of unrealistic expectations and showing willingness to play their part in the overall ministry.

As we turn around some aspects of our lives and practices so God will also turn things around.

Time to turn the tables (Jeremiah 51:11–12)

God's people had been attacked, defeated, taken captive and oppressed by the Babylonians. Jeremiah prophesied a time when the tables would turn on the enemy. It is time in our nations for the tables to turn, for the Church to rise up and the enemy to be put to flight. God will carry out his purpose but he calls us to take our stand and play our part. This is the privilege and responsibility of the servants of God. These verses speak of the battle that is fought to a large extent on the battleground of prayer. The amount we invest in prayer will be crucial. What then do these verses tell us that we need to do?

1. Sharpen the arrows

I believe the arrows speak to us of 'offensive prayer'. The Scriptures use arrows as a symbol of God's means for routing the enemy (Psalm 144:6). In 2 Kings 13 we read of Jehoash, king of Israel, who sought the prophet Elisha's help against his enemies, the Arameans. Elisha tells the king to shoot an arrow out of the window and declares prophetically of this act: *'The LORD's arrow of victory, the arrow of victory over Aram'* (2 Kings 13:17). Elisha then instructs Jehoash to take the arrows and to strike the ground with them. Verse 18 tells us: *'He struck it three times and stopped.'* Elisha becomes angry with the king, telling him that he should have struck the ground five or six times. Elisha was saying that Jehoash showed a lack of spirit and determination so would now only defeat the Arameans three times rather than completely destroying them.

God is looking to raise up offensive warriors who will, at his command, take the battle to the enemy. He seeks those who have the right spirit within them, who will not stop short but will be thorough in routing the enemy strongholds. God is preparing his servants for an onslaught of intercessory prayer that will turn the tables on the powers of darkness. We are too used to talking of enemy onslaughts: it is time we took up our offensive positions to see the Kingdom of God advancing.

Isaiah 49:2 says, *'he made me into a polished arrow and concealed me in his quiver.'* God is preparing his 'arrows' – his prophets and intercessors. Many are as yet concealed in the Lord as he polishes them and makes them ready. He is sharpening us through an increased anointing of insight and revelation from the Holy Spirit. He is preparing our ears to hear and our eyes to see that we might know what to pray, and how to foil and rout the enemy. When doctors see patients they will listen to them describe their symptoms. The doctor may make an educated guess at what is wrong but not be entirely sure. In fact the actual problem can be very different from what the doctor first assumes. The patient may be sent for a scan or an x-ray that shows up exactly what is the cause of the problem. The doctor can then prescribe the necessary course of treatment. We can all see much of what is wrong in our nations and have a reasonable idea of what to pray. However, if we are to be more effective in prayer we need the revelation of the Holy Spirit to expose the root problems and his wisdom to instruct us how we should pray.

God desires to sharpen his people, to make us sharp in the Spirit, alert and ready to respond. The Church needs to be more thoroughly equipped in learning how to *'pray in the Spirit on all occasions'* (Ephesians 6:18). This should not be just a small number of believers but as we invest in prayer we can have a *'full quiver'* (see Psalm 127:3–5). We need to raise up many sons and daughters who will be like 'arrows in the hand'. Then as we battle the enemy for the gates of our towns and cities we will not be put to shame but instead know the victory of the Lord.

2. Take up the shields

The battle for our towns, cities and nations requires an offensive onslaught and also a good defence. A winning football team must have the ability to score goals – good offence or attack – and have a sound defence that concedes few goals. In the Church we must develop both of these aspects. We need good covering prayer to protect those at the front line of the battle. This is where the Body of Christ works together as we pray 'all kinds of prayers.'

God has given us *'the shield of faith, with which you can extinguish all the flaming arrows of the evil one'* (Ephesians 6:16). We need to pray in faith for the protection of other members of the body from the enemy's darts or arrows. Our confidence is in the Lord and he does not want us to be fearful or foolish regarding the power of the enemy. We need not be scared but we do well to take him seriously. His darts are designed to get us to retreat from the battle. They may come in physical attacks and sickness, disturbances to our sleep, temptations, and disruptions in our family situation or people wasting our time. It is important to pray this defensive covering over pastors, church leaders and their families, but also for the intercessors that are engaged in firing sharp arrows at the enemy encampments.

You may not feel you are called to pray in ways that rout the enemy or that you receive any prophetic revelations. You still have a vitally important part to play. Find someone who is 'an offensive intercessor' and pray a covering over them every day. Pray for your pastor and maybe another key church leader in your area. Ask God to guard them and their families, and make yourself available for the Spirit of God to prompt you to pray when needed.

3. Lift up a banner

Prayer is crucial in defeating the enemy but it is not the only weapon God has given us. Praise and the proclamation of the Word of God are also key for victory in the battle. The banner is a battle standard or sign. Psalm 60:4 says, *'for those who fear you, you have raised a banner, to be unfurled against the bow.'* This banner of praise and proclamation of the truth of God is a defence against the lies and deception of the enemy. When we are downcast or lulled into believing things are hopeless, it is this banner that can rescue us.

The banner is far more than a defence. It is a signal of the rallying point for the troops. A clear, anointed word from the Lord will draw God's army together and direct them to put the enemy to flight. Isaiah 11 speaks of God's banner (which is the Lord Jesus himself) being a means of gathering together his scattered and separated people. Under this banner jealousy and hostility among the people of God will vanish, and they will together attack and plunder the enemy (see Isaiah 11:10–14). We see this happen as the churches focus their gaze on the Lord Jesus himself. As we all find our security and identity in him instead of in our ministries, then jealousy, competition and hostility will fade away and vanish. A church united in their love for Christ will not only stand its ground, but will plunder the enemy camp of its prisoners.

The banner is furthermore a sign to the enemy. As we raise the banner of praise it causes the enemy to retreat. Jehoshaphat's army went out to battle holding high the banner of praise and experienced a great victory as the Lord ambushed their enemies throwing them into confusion. The high praises of God will confuse the powers of darkness and severely hinder their operations.

4. Reinforce the guard

One of our main aims at Prayer for the City is to enlist and strengthen intercessors that will persevere in prayer for city-wide transformation. In the past there have often been small bands of prayer warriors here and there. The prayers of these faithful ones are being answered. One of the ways in which the answer is coming is that God is raising up large companies of intercessors – he is reinforcing the guard.

Over the years Helen and I have sought to encourage and equip people with a calling for intercessory prayer, first in our local church, then across the city. This has often been with quite small numbers of people. We have observed the enemy clearly targeting these folks, and have seen quite a few fall away from the ministry of intercession, and sometimes from the Church altogether. We have seen the health of some of those involved deteriorate at times, or tremendous family pressure come in against them. What I believe we need to do is so increase the number of active intercessors that it becomes impossible for the enemy with his finite resources to target them all.

Isaiah 54:11 speaks of the *'afflicted city, lashed by storms'*. That is an apt description of the house of prayer in many places. The enemy has ferociously lashed against those who have heard the call to serious intercessory prayer. He trembles in fear at the thought of a strong, praying church in a city, so he attacks with great venom against the fledgling ministry.

God is faithful, however, and he will rescue us and build his praying Church. The passage in Isaiah goes on to say, *'I will make your battlements of rubies, your gates of sparkling jewels, and all your walls of precious stones'* (Isaiah 54:12). Through all the trials and struggles God is bringing forth his praying children as precious stones. He is cleaning the dirt off and repairing the damage, and with these 'stones' he will build battlements, gates and walls that will make the Church ready for battle and a great day of victory and harvest.

5. Station the watchmen
God has called and posted watchmen on the walls (Isaiah 62:6–7). We need to make sure the watchmen stay in place and keep alert. We have to station or position watchmen in the weak places and where the enemy has entry points to our church and communities. In any city there will be areas where the Church is stronger and areas where it is weaker. Rather than sit comfortably in the stronger areas we need to reposition some of the troops to strengthen the weaker parts.

We need to recognise where the enemy gains access and takes ground in our areas and station the watchmen there to counter what the evil one is doing. We need to be alert to what is going on in our communities. One of the major ills of our city of Glasgow has been bigotry and sectarianism between supposed Protestants and Catholics. This has long historical roots but the problem can be heightened whenever our two major football teams play each other. (One is traditionally a Protestant team, the other Catholic.) We note the dates of these fixtures and get the watchmen stationed ready to counter the spirit that is released through the intense rivalry and sometimes hatred expressed at these events.

6. Prepare an ambush
In some of our towns and cities the enemy has become nonchalant, supposing his strongholds are secure. The Church has rarely disturbed his power base. As the Lord calls forth and raises up an united, believing body of people who will give themselves to extraordinary prayer then the enemy

will be taken by surprise. It is time to be done with half-hearted, timid efforts and rise up in the strength of the Lord to wholehearted, fervent prayer, praise and proclamation that will ambush the works of darkness and open up the way for many captives to come to the Lord.

Conclusion

The Scriptures show us God's ways for breakthrough. We need to seriously invest in prayer so that we have in place a powerful balance of offensive and defensive intercession. For this we need to greatly increase the size of the 'guard' by enlisting and equipping many more prayer warriors, stationing them in the necessary positions. Alongside we need to raise up the banner of Jesus Christ through praising his name and proclaiming his good news.

It is vitally important not to rush forward expecting to reap a harvest without putting these things in place. Once they are, we will see the grace and power of God burst forth in our land as he carries out his glorious purpose.

Notes
1. C. Peter Wagner, *Revival! It Can Transform Your City!* (Wagner Publications, 1999), p. 27.
2. Dutch Sheets, *Watchman Prayer* (Gospel Light, 2000), p. 194.
3. Wagner, ibid. p. 27
4. Wesley Duewel, *Mighty Prevailing Prayer* (Zondervan, 1990), p. 25.
5. I use the term 'pastor' to indicate the key leader in a local church. Some churches depending on their tradition will use various other terms.

Chapter 9

Dynamic Prayer Meetings

In 1990 we began to seriously develop prayer meetings in our small church. As I mentioned in chapter 1 these meetings were generally a small group of 6–12 people meeting either in a home or in our church building. Small numbers are not a hindrance to prayer meetings, in fact the dynamic of a small group – up to about 16–20 people – is often more beneficial for corporate prayer. We maintained the two evenings for a few years before dropping the Saturday and making the Monday our main 'prayer night'. Those Monday evenings became quite special. Over the years the Lord taught us many things, especially to listen to him and rely on his Spirit.

There were some keys that helped to sustain our praying: focus first in worship on seeking God's face and knowing his presence; releasing the anointing of the Spirit on the intercessors; listening to the Lord and praying what he told us; keeping the long-term focus on an ever-increasing outpouring of the Holy Spirit; and all in the context of being a church that is actively reaching out in mission.

Since moving into the ministry of Prayer for the City I have been involved in many prayer meetings of different styles and sizes in various places and would see the following as keys to having and maintaining dynamic, encouraging prayer meetings.

Seven keys

1. Lots of praise and worship – sing to the Lord a new song

It is right and fitting to praise the Lord (Psalm 147:1) and is the most appropriate way to begin any prayer meeting. A constant call of the Scriptures is to sing a new song to the Lord – e.g. Psalm 96:1; 98:1; Revelation 5:9; and it is *'the garment of praise'* (Isaiah 61:3) that is given instead of *'the spirit of heaviness'* (or despair, fainting) as we have previously mentioned. Praising God lifts our soul upwards towards the throne of grace, and brings a renewed perspective on everything as we view our life and circumstances from a place of beholding the majesty of the King.

Praise and worship refreshes the soul. Some of the best experiences of my life have been when gathered with other believers who have a deep desire to worship the Lord and pray together.

Praise in the power of the Spirit binds up any activity of the enemy who seeks to hinder us from prayer (Psalm 149:6–9), and helps create the right conditions for the Holy Spirit to move among us and speak to us. It is good to have an appointed prayer leader who is responsible for the whole meeting, and also to have an appointed praise leader who has prepared well beforehand. It is not to be a matter of preceding prayer with a hymn or song or two, as if to warm us up. The praise is very much an integral and continual part of the meeting. Being well prepared does not, however, need to hinder a spontaneous flow of praise and prayer. In fact quite the opposite can be true. If we are well prepared, not worrying about what to sing or do next, then we can be freer to listen to the Lord and follow the leading of His Spirit. Paul instructs us to *'be filled with the Spirit. Speak to one another with psalms, hymns and spiritual songs'* (Ephesians 5:18–19)

Sometimes a person may complain to a prayer leader that they are spending too much time praising God when the need is to get on with the praying. While we could just keep singing because we like to, it is more often the case that the praises of God's people are leading them into an attitude that is more ready to pray effectively. In fact it is good to keep the spirit of praise going throughout the whole time of prayer, with songs, prayers, prophetic words, and more all flowing together. It is possible to pray at great length and yet have minimum effect (see Matthew 6:7). It is better to honour God in praise and worship, hear what the Spirit of God is saying, and then pray.

2. Encourage hunger and expectancy

After a hard day at work or running after the children we do not always feel full of life and enthusiasm when we come to a prayer meeting. Similarly though we have made the effort to rise early and get to a 6.30 a.m. meeting we may still feel somewhat sleepy. If all in attendance feel that sort of way it is going to be a long and difficult time. We need to encourage and spur one another on. As we pray there needs to be a hunger for God and expectancy for him to answer. We do not falsely manufacture this hunger and expectancy but stir one another up in these ways. Most or all the people there will have a hunger for God's Presence, it may just have had the edge taken off it by the busyness of the day. God is at work and he is answering prayer, but we can lose sight of this. So there is great value in sharing testimony and relating answers to prayer. Take a few minutes to get the enthusiasm for God and his kingdom re-established in the people's hearts.

It will be useful to occasionally make use of specific resources to build up faith afresh. After watching a section of the *Transformations* video we often find the most fervent prayers follow. Just as someone would take time to prepare to lead a Sunday service or to preach, so those leading prayer meetings should take time to prepare themselves and God's people.

3. Pray for the intercessors

Intercessory prayer is hard work and a spiritual battle. We need to cover one another in prayer. I have found it is very helpful to pray over those interceding that the anointing of God would be upon them. This is another way of helping create that hunger we just spoke of and often stirs up the prophetic gift as well.

I have found it useful at times to lay hands on those who have come to pray. I would do this early on in the meeting inviting the Holy Spirit to anoint them for intercession. We are to fan into flame the gift that is in us. I also have felt it is important to pray a covering over those who are praying, and especially when they prophesy or pray prophetically. Those in authority such as pastors or elders, and also husbands covering their wives should do this.

It is often good to pray for each other at the end of the time for refreshment – prayer can take a lot out of us – and for continual protection.

4. Listen to the Holy Spirit

According to Scripture we should eagerly desire prophetic words and prompts (1 Corinthians 14:1). God longs to speak to us, to give us wisdom, and to show us what to pray. Romans 8:26 is such an important verse in relation to prayer stressing our dependence on the Spirit, and therefore produces in us a humble attitude. When we recognise and submit to this truth we can hear what the Spirit is saying to the Church.

Too easily we can charge forward in prayer thinking we are asking for the right things when God is wanting to do something quite different in the situation. Even when the Holy Spirit reveals something for us to pray about we still need to enquire how he wants us to address that situation in our prayers.

Presumption is one of the biggest dangers to us in prayer. David shows a wonderful example of how to wait on the Lord and avoid presumption. We find this in 2 Samuel 5:17–25. The Philistines came against David when he was anointed king over Israel. The expansion of our ministry or authority will often bring an attack of the enemy. What did David do? He enquired of the Lord who instructed him to go and attack the enemy as the Lord's hand was with them. David did so and defeated the Philistines. Once again the same enemy came up against David's position. He could easily have presumed that

God was with him, and as it was the same enemy, the right thing to do would be to attack them as before. Not so. David again takes time to enquire of the Lord who gave him a quite different and unusual strategy to defeat the Philistines this time around. David obeyed and again was victorious.

5. Pray biblical prayers

It is the case that some believers are not sure what to pray for after they have exhausted their list of needs (their own and others known to them). While these petitions are good, and will see many wonderful answers they do not always bring us to the heart of intercessory prayer that the Holy Spirit desires to take us to. It is so important to hear from God (see 4 above) and we have already heard from him through the inspired Word. In Scripture we find many prayers – in the book of Psalms, examples of prayers from other Old Testament characters, such as Nehemiah and Daniel, prayers of Jesus, and the prayers of the apostles and the early Church. Most of these prayers are still being answered, especially those for the Church in the New Testament. For example Paul prayed for the Church to grow in the knowledge of the love of Christ (Ephesians 3:16–19). God was answering that prayer in Paul's day, yet there is still the continual need for the Church to keep growing in this, and so God is still answering this prayer when we pray it today. Indeed these 'apostolic prayers' are prayers that we need to keep praying to see the Church come forth in the fullness of Christ that he desires for his Bride.

Praying scriptural prayers gives us great confidence that God will answer as we are surely praying in line with his will. Examples of scriptural prayers are:

- Old Testament: Psalm 85:4–7; 86:11–13; 144:5–8 and many other Psalms; Isaiah 64:1–2.
- New Testament: Matthew 6:9–13; 9:38.
- Prayers of the apostles for the Church: Acts 4:29–30; Romans 15:5–6; 15:13; Ephesians 1:17–19; 3:16–19; Philippians 1:9–11; Colossians 1:9–13; 1 Thessalonians 3:11–13; 2 Thessalonians 2:16–17; 3:1–5.

- Paul's requests for prayer (pray especially for church leaders): Ephesians 6:19–20; Colossians 4:3–4.

I think it is a good practice to familiarise yourself with these prayers, learning at least a couple off by heart.

6. Stay focused

It is important in corporate prayer times to focus our prayers together in a way that enables us to agree with one another. It is also vital to pray through a need or situation until we believe we have prayed what the Lord would have us pray, and therefore not to jump all over the place. I think it is more beneficial to pray one thing through than to offer up lots of prayers for all sorts of things.

If we come together all having different concerns then we might offer up a lot of prayers but have little agreement. So one person prays for the Sunday service, then someone else jumps in praying for their sick neighbour, and a prayer follows this straight away for a missionary in Zambia. Now these needs and situations are all worthy of prayer but we would do better to stay with one need for a period of time where we can focus together and sense what the Lord is saying about this and what he may want to do. This is where the role of the prayer leader is so crucial. If he lets the praying go all over the place then there will be little cohesion and agreement in our praying. If the prayer leader keeps the people focusing together then the prayers will be more effective.

This will also help us deal with a couple of serious problems that occur too frequently in prayer meetings. First, where people use 'prayer' to put forward their agenda, making their points to us all. Many a good argument has been put forward under the guise of a prayer, and many a church leader has had his or her ministry 'corrected' by such prayers. Second, where people inform the meeting of details about someone or some situation that we really do not need to know about. To explain every detail of some poor soul's troubles to God is quite unnecessary, as he knows all about them anyway.

It can be hard and seem almost insensitive to stop such

'praying' and correct these people. However, we must not let the prayer times be hijacked in such ways, nor should we be willing to allow believers to continue in these practices which are a hindrance to their own growth.

A prayer leader may have to interject every so often to bring the prayers back to the right focal pints. This can and should be done gently, yet firmly, without making it too much of an issue.

7. Link your praying with active mission

It is important that we are praying into the work of mission so that our praying is in line with our commission and purpose to make disciples of all people. We pray for the Church to be built up in the love and fullness of Christ so that we can then more effectively make him known.

We must also back up our prayers with appropriate action. Jesus told his disciples to *'ask the Lord of the harvest . . . to send out workers into his harvest field'* (Matthew 9:38). Straight after this we read of Jesus calling the twelve disciples and sending them out into the harvest field (Matthew 10:1–10). The fact that our Bibles have a chapter division can give the wrong impression that the prayer of 9:38 and the sending out of 10:1–10 are not directly related. (Chapter divisions were not in the original text.) There is no division between praying for a harvest and engaging in the acts of mission to reap that harvest. We need to keep the two linked together. Dutch Sheets comments: 'The way to keep a prayer ministry going is to attach it to the Great Commission.'[1]

Creative prayer

We want our prayer meetings to be effective, and our prayers to produce fruitful results. The preceding keys will help in this as will our ability to involve more people in the actual praying. Therefore developing creative ways of praying will enhance the prayer meeting and release greater potential of fruitful results. We want our prayer meetings to be dynamic and delightful times in God's Presence, rather than dull and difficult occasions where we struggle to get people praying.

God is the Creator and he enables us to be creative in order to enhance worship, prayer and all other ministry. We should not seek to be creative so as to appear trendy or novel but to aid participation and effectiveness.

God-given senses

We have five God-given senses that enable us to look, listen, taste, smell and touch. It is important in our walk with God to cultivate an observant spirit. When Moses saw the burning bush he observed that though it was ablaze the bush was not consumed (Exodus 3:2–3). A burning bush was not an uncommon occurrence in a hot desert, but because Moses was observant he noticed that this bush was different – it did not burn up.

Symbols

Symbols can be of value in praying creatively. In the tradition of Church that I have been most accustomed to there has been little emphasis on the value of symbols, while in other traditions they have been given much more prominence. However, symbols can be powerful means of communication. Various symbolic objects might be used in prayer, such as candles, and we might also use maps of our area, photographs of people we are praying for, and other aids in our praying.

Spiritual gifts

Spiritual gifts are a most valuable resource in prayer as the creative Holy Spirit leads us through prophecy and other means of revelation to pray in most exciting ways.

Song and music

Song and music will enhance our creative abilities and also aid the flow of the gifts of the Holy Spirit. When Elisha was asked to prophesy for the king he first calls for a harpist (2 Kings 3:15). As the harpist begins to pray Elisha is moved by the Spirit of God to prophesy.

Conclusion

The Prayer Meeting can be the most exciting place to be. It need not be 'just another meeting' but a gathering of believers who enter in together to the dynamic and awesome presence of God. There we worship in spirit and in truth, hear his voice and call out in his name. Together we flow in the anointing of the Spirit, in co-operation with him, praying in Jesus' name what he puts in our hearts. These prayers can and will bring incredible and miraculous change to people's lives, to towns, cities and to nations.

Every church should have at least one of these.

Notes:
1. Dutch Sheets, *Watchman Prayer* (Gospel Light, 2000), p. 200.

Chapter 10

Praying Outside the Church

A while ago around 40 churches in our city got together to run an initiative where they held free barbecues in various locations across the area. Thousands of burgers and sausages were given away, praise bands played and sang on the streets and Christians engaged in good conversations with people, even praying with some on the streets. The general feedback from the people was that it was good to see the churches working together and out of their buildings. This was largely a positive experience, except for one or two shops that sold take-away food.

Not all 'open-air' church activities have always been so positive. I was once asked to preach at one such event in the north of Scotland. There had been a fairly tuneless rendering of some old choruses and hymns and it all seemed to be directed at the 'drinkers' in the public house across the road. Some stood outside the pub looking rather disdainfully at us 'holy Joes'. I declined the opportunity to preach and thought that a much better approach may have been to actually talk to and listen to the 'targets' on the other side of the street. Bad experiences may have led us to retreat into the safety of our buildings.

We need to take prayer outside the church. There are times to shut ourselves away in 'a prayer closet' to seek the Lord;

there are many occasions when we need to meet as believers to pray together; and there is also a great need to pray in the streets of our communities and to pray with those who do not yet know Christ.

Prayer walking

What is prayer walking?

Steve Hawthorne and Graham Kendrick produced a book entitled *Prayer-walking* containing the subtitle 'Praying on-site with insight'.[1] This subtitle captures the heart of what prayer walking our communities is all about. It is about getting out and about the streets, in the shopping centres, and around the other places that compose our community, that is getting 'on-site'. Once there we want to pray – observing the goings on and listening to the Holy Spirit – that is the insight.

In our church we did quite a bit of prayer walking of our area. People were often a little apprehensive about it the first time, but afterwards nearly always felt it had been a positive and helpful exercise. As we pray for our city we seek to focus on a certain area each month. We organise a prayer walk with Christians coming from other parts of the city to join with those in that area. It has been a huge help to my understanding of the city to have joined local believers in prayer walking their part of the community.

Why prayer walk?

I have found there to be several real values to prayer walking:

* **We are able to get a better 'feel' of the place**. I often preach in local churches throughout Glasgow. If I drive to the church, park outside and go in and preach, then leave again, I will not get much idea about that area. When I have taken time to walk round the area in an attitude of prayer and seeking to listen to God I have picked up a much greater sense of what that area is about. As we walk slowly and observantly in any place we will notice much that we never observed before.

- **Prayer walks prepare the way for evangelism**. As we prayer walk a street, blessing and interceding for each household we are preparing the way for the work of evangelism to follow. This can also be done by regularly praying through lists of names of families, which can be taken from the voters' role or telephone book. This way those unable to walk the streets can take part. A friend of ours in the Shetland Islands has organised intercessors to pray for every home on the islands by using the voters' role. I have recently heard of a church in Arizona that compiled two lists of names taken from the telephone book. They prayed for ninety days for those on one list but not the other. Then they called every home on both lists offering a call to talk and pray with them. They found a staggering difference. One out of eighty on the list not prayed for was open to such a call, while sixty-nine out of eighty on the list of those prayed for were willing for contact, forty-five of them receiving a home visit.
- **Prayer walking provides some unexpected opportunities**. While out prayer walking I have come across several opportunities to stop and talk with folk that I would not have met otherwise. Sometimes these encounters seemed to be divinely organised. When I have met people I knew they would ask what we were doing. The reply of prayer walking brought occasional raised eyebrows but usually provided the opening to talk about the Lord.

A friend of ours, along with a couple of companions, went out to pray in the grounds of an old cathedral. It was late at night, and as they prayed and worshipped the Lord on this ancient site, they saw three figures appear. They called over to them and it turned out to be three Spaniards who were working in Scotland. They talked about what they were doing and the opportunity opened up to pray with the three visitors in a quite powerful way.

How do we prayer walk?
It can be done on your own but is often best in pairs or small

groups of three to four. If there are a lot of you then split into suitably sized groups. Prayer walking is a simple exercise and should be undertaken in as natural a way as possible.

Obviously keep your eyes open, not just to avoid collisions, but to see what is going on around you. I believe we need to pray with open eyes much more than we often do. Pray out loud just as if you were talking to each other in the group, but try to avoid actually spending too much of the time chatting to one another.

Pay attention to what the Holy Spirit may be pointing out to you and make notes when you are finished walking.

Focus more on blessing your neighbourhood and praying in the light of Christ rather than coming against every work of the evil one.

When should we prayer walk?

- **Regularly**. It is good to make it a regular practice. You might prayer walk your own street every day or once a week. A church group might walk a number of the streets in their area once a month. It is good to take a sense of responsibility for your area and the best thing you can do is to pray for it.
- **Before seeking to evangelise a street or area**. As we have already said, prayer walking opens up the way for the evangelists to come into a place.
- **When there has been a rise in violence or other destructive works in a place**. When there has been a spate of trouble in a specific place, or some serious crime or even murder has occurred, then it is vitally important for the Christians to get active in countering these destructive forces with on the spot prayer.

Some time ago we went to minister in a town in the south of Scotland. While driving into the area and again when leaving we sensed a strong oppressive power. About a year later we took a team back to that town. This time we felt the oppression had lifted and there was a real peace on entering the area. In the church that morning a lady told us how she had been spending much of the last year walking dogs (she looks after people's pets as a job) round the outskirts of the town and praying as she went. She asked if this was the sort of thing she should be doing. We assured her it was and were sure her regular prayer walking was making a big difference.

Praying with unbelievers

We too often take our theology of the gifts of the Spirit from 1 Corinthians where Paul is writing to correct some excesses, and deal with their use in the church gathering. We need to develop a balanced theology by considering the use of gifts in the Gospels and Acts. Works of healing and miracles are not primarily intended for church meetings but for the Church's mission.

The Holy Spirit and his power were given to the Church so we could be witnesses for Christ to the ends of the earth (Acts 1:8). In the book of Acts we see many miraculous occurrences that were associated with the impact and growth of the early Church.

Power encounters in Acts

By using the term 'power encounter' I mean an incident where the power of God is demonstrated as superior to the powers of this fallen world and the power of the demonic forces, leading to healing, liberty and other positive effects.

1. Power encounters often preceded preaching

Acts 14:3 speaks of the signs and wonders confirming the word, and Mark 16:17 similarly states that signs will accompany those who preach. This has sometimes been interpreted as 'signs following' the preaching of the word. This is not necessarily the case, and when we look at the whole of Acts it appears more often that the signs preceded the preaching. In fact on numerous occasions the miracle or sign opened up the opportunity for the apostles to preach to a ready made and attentive audience (see for example Acts 2:4–41; 3:1–26; 8:4–8). Miracles provide a platform for the message.

How we need this today in our society. The vast majority of people in our land are not listening to the Church. We need to get their attention. One way is through sacrificial acts of love and service; another is through signs, wonders and healings:

> *'When the crowd heard Philip and saw the miraculous signs he did, they all paid close attention to what he said.'* (Acts 8:6)

2. Power encounters were usually in the open

While miracles and healings take place in the Church and among the believers, most of what we read of in Acts is very much in the public domain. Peter and John heal the crippled man at a gate outside the Temple (3:2), and the sick are brought into the streets so that Peter's shadow might fall on them (5:15). Miracles take place on the streets, in the market place, in homes and even in jails. They continually occur among those who were at the time outside the Church.

I believe that we would see many more genuine healings if we took this ministry out of the church a lot more. The power of God is not to be hidden away – it is to be a sign that points to Jesus.

3. Power encounters led to transformation

In Acts 9:32–43 we read of whole villages turning to the Lord after dramatic, public miracles took place. Philip's ministry in Samaria caused the whole city to be filled with great joy. It is not just the person healed who was affected but many people around them are stirred to faith as a result of these miracles. In each of these cases the power of God, in the name of Jesus Christ, was being demonstrated as the true power to heal, set free and give new life. His power is surely the same today and can have the same effects.

4. Power encounters also led to persecution

When God's power is let loose the enemy gets seriously worried. His captives are being set free and his holds are breaking apart. It is not unusual then that with power encounters comes persecution. We see this in 4:1–22 where it is the religious leaders of the Jews who persecute the apostles. We can find that there may be some in the church who will come against us when we start praying for the sick. They may speak against us, disagreeing because of their theological perspective, or others may even speak out of jealousy. The enemy will use any mouthpiece he can get.

In Acts 16:16–24 and again in 19:23ff. it is the pagan worshippers who bring the opposition, though primarily because they are going to lose money due to the apostles' ministry. In 13:4–12 we see the opposition of a sorcerer against Paul's testimony to the proconsul in Cyprus. A power encounter follows which reveals clearly the power of Paul's God. Today there are those with allegiance to the powers of darkness through occult practices who will seek to threaten the ministry of those moving in the power of the Holy Spirit.

Paul's perspective that we read in 1 Corinthians 16:8–9 is very interesting:

> *'I will stay on in Ephesus until Pentecost, because a great door for effective work has opened to me, and there are many who oppose me.'*

The two tend to go together – opportunity and opposition – the first should spur us on, and the second in no way should put us off.

5. The apostles prayed for power encounters

Healings and miracles did not just happen. The apostles had to be filled with the Spirit and get out with the good news. They also prayed for more miracles and healings. In the face of opposition they ask God to *'enable them to speak the word with great boldness.'* They knew that they needed more than that and continued to ask the Lord to *'stretch out his hand to heal and perform miraculous signs and wonders through the name of Jesus'* (Acts 4:29–30). The result of this prayer was a shaken building and a fresh infilling of the Spirit, leading to the bold proclamation of God's Word. We have made this apostolic prayer one of the key prayers we cry out repeatedly for our city.

Developing the practice of praying with unbelievers

I believe that the Lord wants his Church today to similarly rise up and proclaim the good news. Like the early Church we need this to be aided by the power of prayer and signs, wonders and miracles.

There has been much prayer for the sick and expectation of miracles in some sectors of the Church. There have been some wonderful healings and miracles among believers. There has also been some frustration and disappointment at times. I believe this frustration will continue to be the case unless we get the message that power encounters are primarily for the work of mission, and that we need to be praying with unbelievers for healing and miracles.

I have prayed for the sick for many years. I took the decision to keep doing so based on the Word of God, not on the results. Jesus told, in fact commanded, his disciples to preach the good news, heal the sick and drive out demons (see Luke 9:1–2; 10:9). I have prayed for many Christians and will continue to do so. I have witnessed a few being healed, many feeling a definite benefit, while many times nothing appears to have happened at all.

I have prayed for quite a number of people who were not Christians. Most have been completely healed, including tumours 'vanishing'. Some have felt great benefit and sensed the love and peace of God in a tangible way. Virtually none have failed to experience a definite benefit. I now am actively seeking every opportunity to offer to pray with unbelievers.

Some Christians may think it would be difficult or awkward to pray with someone who is not yet a Christian, supposing such a person would not be open to prayer, especially with the laying on of hands. I have found almost the opposite to be the case. Very few such people who have an illness or serious problem tend to refuse the offer of prayer. Even if they have no faith they believe that we as Christians do. Some are a little surprised when told that I will pray with them right there and then, but if this is done sensibly and sensitively then there is rarely any objection. They have nothing to lose. Those outside of the Church are much more open to spiritual reality and the potential power of prayer than many Christians think. They are also often very willing to receive prayer for their needs, and delighted that someone would take the time to pray with them.

With so much need in our world, so many sick people, and so many suffering from addictions it would seem the most natural thing for the Church to pray for them. We need to do so naturally yet supernaturally as we invite the power of the Holy Spirit to touch people's lives. And the Holy Spirit loves to take up that invitation. I have seen numerous unbelievers moved to tears as the Spirit of God descends upon them. They do not understand it but know it is real. We can then explain it to them.

Not all who are prayed for and experience healing or some other miracle necessarily become Christians. Some do, some will later on and some may not. Nevertheless such power encounters open many doors for the good news causing people to pay close attention to what we have to say about Jesus.

Where do we pray with unbelievers?
It could be in church buildings at times, for example at special healing services or other occasions. Some people will come to such events, especially where they have some relationship with us, but there are many folks who are unlikely to come to our buildings. So we also need to go out and pray with people wherever the opportunity arises. This may be in homes, on the streets, in workplaces, hospitals or almost anywhere.

Often it is good not to be on 'church territory' but on occasions where we have made appointments to pray with someone with great need, for example major health issues, then it is good to have a place where we can minimise disruptions.

How to pray for unbelievers
This will not be very different from praying with those who are already Christians. I always recommend that a woman is

present if a woman is being prayed for, and similarly a man present if a man is being prayed for.

1. **Explain what you are going to do.** If you think you may lay hands on them, let them know why you will do this and then do it in a sensitive manner. Help them to relax and be prepared to receive from God. Explain anything you might do such as praying in tongues.
2. **Pray simply and naturally.** Do not use religious talk and Christian jargon. Do not pray in a way that implies you are passing any judgement on their condition. Simply invite the Lord to touch them, heal them or do whatever is needed. Trust God to do it.
3. **See what happens and respond to it.** If they start to experience something, for example heat, or they begin to fall down, then reassure them that this is okay, and that it is a sign of God at work. Bless what you see the Father doing (as John Wimber used to say).
4. **Point them toward Jesus as Lord and Saviour.** As they experience something of God's power in their life explain that this comes from a real, personal God who loves them and longs to bring them into relationship with himself. However, do not push too much. They may experience God's power or even healing, but not yet be ready to commit their life to Christ. This may just be one step in several that are often needed before true conversion. Beware of trying to pick unripe fruit.

Healing as a sign of the Kingdom

When asked if he was the Messiah by John the Baptist's disciples, Jesus replied:

> *'Go back and report to John what you have seen and heard: The blind receive sight, the lame walk, those who have leprosy are cured, the deaf hear, the dead are raised, and good news is preached to the poor.'*   (Luke 7:22)

These were the signs of the Kingdom, the rule of God.

I believe that God wants to restore this understanding to the Church in this day, that healing is a sign of the Kingdom. Instead of healing meetings being full of believers looking for that touch of God that will change everything (they think), we need to get healing out among those who are perishing that they might see this sign and turn to the King.

Note
1. Steve Hawthorne and Graham Kendrick *Prayer-Walking* (Creation House, 1993).

Conclusion

Prayer is all about expressing our relationship with the Father. It is first of all about **delighting** in the Lord and as we do so we will **desire** to know him more.

As we grow in our knowledge of him so we will grow in our love for him and for his will to be done. This will lead us into intercessory prayer that is **desperate** for his Kingdom to come and **determined** to see it increase. In this growing relationship we realize more and more our **dependence** on his Spirit and our need to be **disciplined** in prayer.

These are the ingredients for breakthrough prayer. Our world desperately needs people whose lives incorporate these ingredients. It will be through such praying people and praying churches that transformed lives and communities will come about.

To see such breakthrough we need the united Church in our towns and cities to be moving forward in the following process:

* **Preparing the Church**. Preparing a people who are devoted to the Lord, growing in an understanding of his ways, and being equipped for works of ministry. Not only does the Church need to be equipped in the sense of being trained, but also the Church needs encouraged and built up in an expectant faith.

- **Being a praying Church**. Becoming and being a Church filled with believers who have strong personal prayer lives. This in turn will increasingly lead to dynamic corporate prayer and the releasing of prayer onto the streets of our communities.
- **A Church with presence in the city**. This sustained prayer walking should be accompanied by Christians being involved in serving their local communities in practical demonstrations of God's love, and by a visible worshipping presence in the community.
- **A Church showing God's power**. The Church being out in the community in the ways mentioned above will lead to opportunities to pray with unbelievers resulting in healing, signs and wonders. Such evidence of God's power will open the way for powerful, life-changing ministries among the most needy and desperate of our society.

This will all result in the **proclamation** of the good news, not preaching angrily at 'the sinners out there' but sharing the life-transforming message of God's grace to those who are willing to listen because they have seen something of the demonstration of the power and compassion of Christ.

Finally this must lead to **planting** new churches. We should not always try and get new believers into our church, but maybe build new churches round them – in 'their house' so to speak. We see this pattern with Matthew's house and the party he holds for Jesus (Matthew 9:9–13). We need to take church to those we are reaching out to and be prepared to explore various models of how we might plant church in this day.

While this whole process will require a significant proportion of the church in the community to be actively involved, it begins with, and is empowered by, individuals who have grasped a vision from the Lord and set themselves to pray resolutely for breakthrough.

Recommended Reading

Beckett, Bob, *Commitment to Conquer*, Chosen Books, 1997.

Bickle, Mike, *Passion for Jesus*, Kingsway Publications, 1993.

———, *The Pleasures of Loving God*, Creation House, 2000.

Chavda, Mahesh, *The Hidden Power of Prayer and Fasting*, Destiny Image, 1998.

Duewel, Wesley L., *Mighty Prevailing Prayer*, Francis Asbury/ Zondervan, 1990.

Frangipane, Francis, *The House of the Lord*, New Wine Press, 1991.

Goll, Jim W. *Kneeling on the Promises*, Chosen Books, 1999.

———, *The Lost Art of Intercession*, Destiny Image, 1997.

Hawthorne, Steve, and Graham Kendrick, *Prayer-Walking*, Creation House, 1993.

Otis, George, Jr, *Informed Intercession*, Gospel Light Books, 1999.

Sheets, Dutch, *Intercessory Prayer*, Gospel Light, 1996.

———, *Watchman Prayer*, Gospel Light, 2000.

Silvoso, Ed, *Prayer Evangelism*, Gospel Light, 2000.

Wagner, C. Peter, *Revival! It Can Transform Your City*, Wagner Institute, 1999.

———, *Warfare Prayer*, Regal, 1992.